THE WIZARD'S COOKBOOK

ACKNOWLEDGMENTS

•■•

Because this book would not be what it is without them,
I want especially to thank:

all those who, with their professionalism,
talent, and creativity, have brought these pages to life;
Didier, who was the first to believe in this book, and Corinne;
Marjorie, for her great ideas at just the right time;
Peter and Alexia for their photographs and styling;
Moshi Moshi Studio for their graphic design;
Liguori for his help with *Doctor Strange* and *Warcraft*;
the team at Le Relais Bernard Loiseau for their geat kindness and generosity with their
time; the team in charge of the youth section of the Bayeux Municipal Library;
Laurence, for her unfailing enthusiasm;
Lina, Naël, and Elian for their spontaneous comments and contagious good humor;
Yannick and Yannaëlle, whose friendship has buoyed me up;
C., P., Ch., E., and O., thank you for being you, thank you for being there;
Cyril and Emily for their love, their humor . . . and their patience;
and, above all, you, the reader, without whom nothing would be possible.

Aurélia Beaupommier

THE WIZARD'S COOKBOOK

Magical Recipes Inspired by
Harry Potter, Merlin, The Wizard of Oz,
and More

Skyhorse Publishing

Visit our website at www.skyhorsepublishing.com.

10 9 8 7 6 5

Library of Congress Cataloging-in-Publication Data is available on file.

Cover design by Michael Short
Cover artwork by Moshi Moshi Studio

ISBN: 978-1-5107-2924-7
eISBN: 978-1-5107-2928-5

Printed in China

PREFACE

This book is the result of a conversation between friends.
Nibbling on a small piece of cake one day, one friend remarked that it was worthy of Mary Poppins, another suggested that Gandalf might have preferred sipping a little pick-me-up to eating cake, while a third friend pointed out that the White Witch of Narnia excelled at making enchanted Turkish delight.

This exchange piqued my curiosity and an idea started
running around in my head: when witches and wizards aren't busy casting spells, saving the world, or plotting sinister schemes, what do they like to eat? It sparked an investigation that proved to be enthralling. Refusing to be intimidated by piles of dusty books of spells, browsing miles of shelving, and viewing many hours of film and television series, I found many djinn, magicians, fairies, witches, and wizards of all shapes and sizes who would let me in on the secrets of their small treats and great feasts, and shared with me the secrets of their grimoires—magic textbooks. And while some recipes have been inspired by the various universes the magicians inhabit, the great majority have been taken directly from their adventures.

From the Babylon of Bartimaeus, 3,000 years ago, to Circe,
the interstellar sorceress of *Ulysses 31*, from the ubiquitous Harry Potter to Puck, the impish nocturnal wanderer from *A Midsummer Night's Dream,* from traditional fairy tales (*The Snow Queen, Snow White*) to today's superheroes (Doctor Strange), not forgetting the magicians of the digital universe (*World of Warcraft*) and the familiar faces of the big and small screens, I invite you to discover the tasty dishes of all of these magical beings.

To make things easier, this book has been divided into main chapters.
The first covers everyday cooking, the food we serve without fanfare to friends and family, which is easy to put together with the usual contents of a modern sorcerer's cupboard. The second fits the small dishes into larger ones and lets you create feasts for sorcerers of all ages. The third chapter is given over to sweet treats and small indulgences, since magic and decadence have been inseparable since the dawn of time. Finally, the last section is devoted to the art of potions, those precious elixirs that sorcerers put to many different uses.

Now it is your turn to savor this book and the wonderful stories
behind the recipes. Don't hesitate. Pick up your wand, get your best cauldrons out of the cupboard, and remember, above all:
"Those who don't believe in magic will never find it." (Roald Dahl)

Aurélia Beaupommier

ALADDIN

Aladdin, a boy from the poor part of town and hero of the tales of the *One Thousand and One Nights*, meets a powerful sorcerer named Jafar. Jafar asks him to fetch from a mysterious cave a humble lamp that he is unable to reach himself. Aladdin is suspicious and refuses to hand over the lamp until Jafar helps him out of the Cave of Wonders. Furious, the sorcerer shuts Aladdin in the cave, which is why, in need of light, Aladdin rubs the lamp and discovers it houses a genie who can fulfill his wildest dreams with his extraordinary powers. But Jafar wants to get the lamp back and will stop at nothing to use the powers of the genie to his own advantage.

Recipes on pages 19, 20, 21, 125, 126, 173.

THE BARTIMAEUS TRILOGY

The *Bartimaeus Trilogy* is a series of novels published between 2003 and 2005 by Jonathan Stroud. Bartimaeus, a djinni who is some five thousand years old, irreverent, sarcastic, and in possession of a caustic sense of humor, is summoned up in the London of the twentieth century by Nathaniel, a gifted young magician. Bartimaeus will help him evade the traps and unravel the plot cooked up by a dark magician, Simon Lovelace. Later on, Nathaniel, now John Mandrake and the youngest Minister in history, finds Bartimaeus again, who is in better shape than ever to deal with a formidable conspiracy mixing treacherous magicians, powerful demons, indestructible golems, and stubborn rebels.

Recipes on pages 33, 34, 36, 69, 70, 119, 120, 168.

ASTERIX AND OBELIX

Getafix is the resident druid in Asterix's small village in Gaul, described in cartoon form by René Goscinny and Albert Uderzo. The village is famous for forever resisting the Roman invaders. Dressed in a venerable white tunic to match his equally venerable beard, along with sandals and a red cape, as wise as he is knowledgable, you would never start out on an adventure without first consulting Getafix. It is Getafix who prepares the famous magic potion—whose secret recipe can only be passed down through the druids by word of mouth!—which gives superhuman strength to those who drink it, allows the villagers to fight their enemies, and lets Asterix and Obelix overcome many perilous predicaments.

Recipes on pages 93, 175.

BEAUTY AND THE BEAST

Transformed into a bestial creature as punishment for his selfishness, the prince shuts himself away in his palace until the day a poor merchant who has lost his way asks the Beast for shelter. The next morning, the merchant picks a pink rose from the palace garden as a gift for his daughter, Beauty. It provokes the wrath of the Beast, who demands that Beauty comes to live in the castle as punishment for her father's theft. Living together in the strange house, which is inhabited by invisible servants and where dishes appear and disappear like magic, Beauty and the Beast come over time to know and love each other, thus breaking the spell. This tale, whose oldest version dates back to the second century, has been brought to the screen numerous times, including most recently the 2017 adaptation starring Emma Watson.

Recipes on pages 99, 101.

BEWITCHED

In this series, first broadcast on television in 1964, Samantha is a witch who has lived incognito for many centuries among humans and who then marries Darrin, a 1960s advertising man who knows nothing about the existence of witches. The couple would enjoy a life of unclouded bliss—if Samantha's mother Endora did not contrive to make Darrin's life impossible with her spells; if their daughter Tabitha could stop herself from using her powers in the presence of the neighbors; or if magic-induced disasters did not constantly disturb their not-so-peaceful existence. Fortunately, thanks to her powers and sense of humor, Samantha always manages to fix things with a twitch of her nose.

Recipes on pages 42, 65, 67, 137.

DOCTOR STRANGE

In this comic book by Stan Lee and Steve Ditko, Stephen Strange has risen rapidly to become the world's best neurosurgeon but he does not handle the success associated with this meteoric rise well. He becomes selfish and arrogant, letting patients suffer in favor of wealthier clients who can afford his services. Following a car accident that damages his hands, he loses his legendary dexterity. Strange feels his life is ruined and plunges into a deep depression. He then hears about a Tibetan healer, the Ancient One, who could be his last chance. A master of the occult sciences, the Ancient One does not cure Strange but trains him in magic to make him a powerful sorcerer.

Recipes on pages 58, 105.

BROCÉLIANDE FOREST

Merlin, called "The Enchanter," stands out as one of the most famous wizards of all time. A whimsical magician, he knows everything about everything, commands the elements and animals alike, is fond of games and pranks, and is a shapeshifter and astronomer. A tireless time traveler, he is said to have had a hand in facilitating the construction of Stonehenge, King Arthur's accession to the throne with his famous sword Excalibur, and the creation of the legendary Round Table. Viviane, or the Lady of the Lake, makes Lancelot a knight and protects King Arthur. It is also said that, in love with the Enchanter Merlin, she had him drink a love potion and, because of it, he will now live forever in Brocéliande forest.

Recipes on pages 138, 149.

DUNGEONS & DRAGONS

A tabletop role-playing game later adapted into video games and movies, the world of *Dungeons & Dragons* has also inspired many fantasy novels. The heroes, represented by the players, exist in medieval fantasy worlds where they go on quests, solve puzzles, thwart plots, or confront curses that have been placed on them. The characters belong to different races (elves, dwarves . . .), and have various occupations (thieves, warriors . . .), but have personalities ranging from very good to utterly evil. Their actions and experience thus have different repercussions and affect the game play.

Recipes on pages 47, 87, 89, 91, 145, 176.

FANTASTIC BEASTS

A sorcerer from the world of J. K. Rowling, Newt Scamander is a "magizoologist," a specialist in magical creatures, and also an alumnus of the Hogwarts School of Witchcraft and Wizardry. In the early twentieth century Newt travels over hill and dale to create a bestiary cataloguing magical creatures and their habitats and behaviors. Several animals escape when he makes a stopover in New York, risking exposing the magical community.

Recipes on pages 64, 113.

GOOSEBUMPS

To read R. L. Stine's *Goosebumps* series is to enter into bewitched worlds populated by terrifying creatures (ghosts, werewolves . . .) who lurk in the most unexpected places (mirrors, clocks . . .) or else right next to you (at the museum, fairground . . .). Among them is "Mr. Bad Boy," the evil ventriloquist's doll Slappy the Dummy. Carved from the cursed wood of a wizard's coffin, he only comes to life when someone reads the mysterious phrase written on a piece of paper in his jacket pocket. Slappy then won't rest until he has enslaved his new master, or, as in the 2015 film, tries to set free all of the monsters contained in the books of the series.

Recipes on pages 83, 96, 117, 177.

HALLOWEEN

Also called "Samhain," this pagan festival is celebrated on October 31, the eve of All Saints' Day. For sorcerers it is the equivalent of New Year's Day for humans, albeit with magical powers. Very popular in the magical community, Halloween is an occasion for gatherings, bonfires, and feasts, where there is singing and dancing until morning, sometimes in the company of a few spirits of the dead. This vital celebration within the magical community is also much celebrated by children, when it is an occasion to swap tricks for treats.

Recipes on pages 23, 73, 133, 165.

HARRY POTTER

A series of novels by J. K. Rowling adapted to film, this saga recounts the adventures of a young orphan boy who one fine day discovers a world of whose existence he was hitherto unaware. Not only does he learn that he has magical powers, but also that he is the Chosen One awaited by an entire wizarding community to defeat the most powerful dark wizard of all time, and murderer of his parents, Lord Voldemort. At Hogwarts, he learns magic and forms a tight bond with his friends Ron Weasley and Hermione Granger and they become an inseparable trio, whether joking with the impressive but kindly headmaster Albus Dumbledore, or having to attending the potion class of the somber Professor Snape.

Recipes on pages 75, 76, 115, 121, 155, 157.

THE LEGEND OF ZELDA

Link is the hero of *The Legend of Zelda* video game series. A native of Hyrule and recognizable by his tunic and green cap, he fights valiantly against the forces of evil to come to the aid of Princess Zelda and save the kingdom of Hyrule. Even though his sword and shield are always by his side, he is perfectly adept with a sometimes surprising set of weapons (boomerang, ocarina . . .). He draws his powers from the Triforce, the relic concentrating the power of the gods, of which he holds the Courage segment.
Recipe on page 159.

THE LION KING

Rafiki is the great shaman of the Pride Lands. The old mandrill—wise, experienced, and sometimes eccentric —advises the animals and the King, guiding them to consider the right questions, both for themselves and for the welfare of all the animals of the Pride Lands. This animated film, inspired by Osamu Tezuka's manga comic *Kimba the White Lion* and William Shakespeare's classic play *Hamlet*, takes us deep into the heart of the power struggles, rituals, and superstitions of the savanna.
Recipe on page 63.

THE LORD OF THE RINGS

In the universe created by J. R. R. Tolkien, Gandalf, an immensely knowledgeable wizard, friend of the hobbits, and leader of the Fellowship of the Ring, is the formidable adversary of Sauron and Saruman. The latter is a white wizard who was sent to Middle-earth to fight against Sauron before his ambition led him to succumb to the mirages of the master of Mordor. Radagast the Brown is a wizard living on the edge of Mirkwood. While he supports the fight against Sauron, he prefers the company of animals and plants to men. Beorn meanwhile is able to take the form of a giant black bear. He lives between Mirkwood and the Misty Mountains, which he protects from goblins and orcs. The Ents for their part are the powerful and ancient guardians of the trees of Middle-earth.
Recipes on pages 27, 29, 31, 123, 151, 152, 153.

MAGICA DE SPELL

The relentless Magica De Spell is a duck-witch and sworn enemy of Uncle Scrooge. Originally from the slopes of Vesuvius, where her lair is located, she is relentless in her attempts to make herself rich by every magical and alchemical means at her disposition, including black magic. Her dream is to steal Scrooge's Number One Dime—the first dime earned by the richest duck in the world!—so she can melt it into an amulet that would bring her a fortune greater than the famous Balthazar. And nothing will stop her from reaching this goal! Not even a trip back through time.
Recipes on pages 51, 129.

MARY POPPINS

With her parrot umbrella, prim hat bearing flowers and cherries, carpetbag, and excellent letters of reference, Mary Poppins seems the most respectable of nannies. From the moment she arrives at the Banks' family home at 17 Cherry Tree Lane, however, her methods seem rather unconventional. The children's room tidies itself up while Mary whistles like a robin. When she takes the children to the park, she leads them inside chalk pictures drawn by her friend Bert, where they spend a day having adventures in a magical world. A visit to an old uncle ends in laughter while taking tea on the ceiling and an innocent stroll becomes a wild jig across the rooftops of London. This novel by P. L. Travers was made into a film in 1964.

Recipes on pages 39, 111, 112, 160.

MELUSINE

Melusine is a legendary witch who comes in many different guises. She can be found in different regions of France, where she often takes on the appearance of a woman, but she can also transform herself at will into a snake or bird. You can find her on some nights busy building cities and houses by the light of the moon. They say that, struck by a curse, she was condemned to hide from her husband one day a week, when she took the form of a snake below the waist. You can also find Melusine inside the squares of a comic strip, where she is a young red-haired witch who divides her time between a Transylvanian castle, where she works as an au pair, and a witches school, where she is a diligent student, aware of her special gifts.

Recipe on page 130.

A MIDSUMMER NIGHT'S DREAM

Puck is a mischievous and rebellious elf, a favorite of Oberon, the King of the Fairies. Able to take on the appearance of creatures that can be terrifying or amusing, cunning or friendly, he likes to have fun playing tricks and leading travelers astray in the night. Titania is the Queen of the Fairies, elves, and goblins. In William Shakespeare's *A Midsummer Night's Dream*, she is the wife of Oberon. Having provoked Oberon's jealousy and anger, he orders Puck to cast a spell on the Queen, which will make her fall in love with the first creature she sees, even if it is a donkey.

Recipe on page 140.

NANNY MCPHEE

Mr. Brown's seven children, who recently lost their mother, have made frightening their nannies their specialty. But the Nanny McPhee of the film, Nurse Matilda in the novels by Christianna Brand, is no ordinary nanny: dressed in black, with a warty face, a crooked nose, and always carrying her cane, everything about her is like a witch, including her powers. Of course, the children try to resist her, but when they are muted when they want to speak and compelled to be polite, it soon becomes more fun to do what she says. Especially because Nanny McPhee, beneath her stern exterior, turns out to be a very valuable ally when a strange woman sets her sights on marrying Mr. Brown.

Recipes on pages 41, 109.

SLEEPING BEAUTY

Offended at not having been invited to the baptism of the daughter of King Stefan, Maleficent (also known as the wicked fairy godmother in the version of the story by Charles Perrault) condemns Princess Aurora to prick her finger on the spindle of a spinning wheel on her sixteenth birthday, and thus sink into an eternal sleep which can only be broken by true love's kiss. Surrounding the castle with impenetrable brambles, she jealously guards the princess, not hesitating to take the form of a dragon if necessary to fight those who want to steal Aurora away.

Recipe on page 163.

THE SMURFS

With his cat Azrael always by his side, Gargamel hunts down Smurfs because they are the essential ingredient for making the Philosopher's Stone. If only he could catch them! This however is not going to happen any time soon, because no one can find Smurf village unless they are guided there by one of its inhabitants. Papa Smurf is distinguished by his cap, red pants, and venerable white beard, along with his ability to speak the language of humans. The energetic leader of the small blue gnomes is 542 years old, giving him the necessary wisdom and experience to avoid the traps set for them by the scheming Gargamel in the forty-odd volumes of this Belgian comic created by the cartoonist Peyo.

Recipes on pages 84, 167.

THE SNOW QUEEN

There are several versions of Hans Christian Andersen's fairy tale. One of them features two sisters, one of whom can command ice and cold. In the traditional version, the Snow Queen is riding her sleigh and kidnaps Kai, a young boy, to take him back to her ice palace. There, she freezes his heart to make him lose all memory of his family and his friend Gerda so that he will stay with her forever. Gerda, who has gone looking for Kai, narrowly escapes a witch and finds him imprisoned in the palace. Taking advantage of the Queen's absence, Gerda enters the castle and frees her friend by melting the ice that has frozen his heart and mind.

Recipe on page 53.

SNOW WHITE
AND THE SEVEN DWARFS

Obsessed by her beauty and terribly jealous of Snow White, the Wicked Queen decides to get rid of her by having her killed by a huntsman. Snow White finds refuge in the forest, prompting the Queen to change strategy. Helped by her magic mirror, the Wicked Queen transforms herself into an ugly old woman, finds Snow White, and offers her a poisoned apple. This fairy tale, collected by the Brothers Grimm and published for the first time in 1812, is said to have been inspired by a German myth.

Recipes on pages 107, 164.

ULYSSES 31

In the animated television series *Ulysses 31*, first shown in France in 1981, which follows the broad outlines of Homer's *Odyssey* in a futuristic setting, Circe is a an enchantress who aims to gather together all of the knowledge, stories, and legends that have been told since the origin of the worlds. She lures the crews of passing spaceships and charms them during an elaborate banquet, then hypnotizes them so they stay forever by her side and help her manage her intergalactic library.

Recipe on page 135.

WILLOW

Willow Ufgood, the hero of the film *Willow*, directed in 1988 by Ron Howard, is a Nelwyn (little person) living modestly with his family on a small farm, cherishing the hope of one day becoming a great sorcerer. One morning his children find a human baby on the riverbank. The village council assigns him the task of taking the little girl to a crossroads and entrusting her to the first Daikini (human) he meets. This is how Willow makes the acquaintance of Madmartigan, a disreputable mercenary but excellent warrior. Saving the sorceress Fin Raziel along their way, who teaches him the art of magic, Willow and Madmartigan lead Elora toward her destiny: to shatter the reign of the tyrannical Bavmorda.

Recipe on page 95.

THE WITCHES

According to Roald Dahl's novel *The Witches*, they live among us as quite ordinary women, far from the popular image we have of them. But if you pay attention, the gloves they always wear, their lack of toes, and their bald heads hidden under wigs should tip you off. They lurk everywhere, especially in England, and desperately seek to eliminate children, by all possible means. Led by the Grand High Witch, they gather together in a large hotel, where they try to pass unnoticed. But a young boy sees right through them and infiltrates their Meeting.

Recipe on page 45.

THE WIZARD OF OZ

Dorothy is torn from her home by a violent tornado that rages over Kansas. With her little dog Toto, she arrives in the Land of Oz, where she is told that only the great Wizard living in the Emerald City can get her back home. Along the way, Dorothy meets a scarecrow who would like to be smart, a lion who seeks courage, and a tin woodman who longs for a heart. Together they head to the Emerald City, but the road turns out to be strewn with dangers orchestrated by the wicked witches of Oz. The 1900 novel by L. Frank Baum was released as a film in 1939, starring Judy Garland, and won the Academy Award that year for best song, "Over the Rainbow."

Recipes on pages 54, 57.

THE WORLD OF NARNIA

According to C. S. Lewis, the author of this novel saga, it was quite by chance that Digory and his friend Polly created Narnia, by playing with magic rings. Jadis, the White Witch, is a terrifying sorceress, half-giant, half-djinn. Awakened by Digory, she arrives in Narnia shortly afterward, where she reigns for a hundred years, ensuring that it is "always winter and never Christmas." Fought against by Peter, Susan, Edmund, and Lucy Pevensie, she is defeated by Aslan at the Battle of Beruna. It is her sister who sends Eustace and his companions to the Harfang Giants for their Autumn Feast. During their exploration of the Lone Islands, the crew of the *Dawn Treader* face many magical phenomena, including the cave that turns those who fall asleep in it into a dragon and Dufflepud Island.
Recipes on pages 25, 26, 77, 78, 81, 143, 169, 171.

WORLD OF WARCRAFT

Once upon a time there was a video game set in Azeroth, a fantasy world populated by many mythical races. Each of them is in search of quests and instances to successfully complete for the power, glory, and many treasures promised to the victors. To defeat your enemies, everything is a matter of choice: join the Alliance or the Horde? Become a renowned warrior or a dreaded shaman? What skills do you need to develop to become essential in a guild? Each player has to confront these questions every day before forging the right alliances and engaging in brutal, epic, and legendary battles.
Recipe on page 48.

MAGICAL FOOD
FOR
EVERYDAY

ALADDIN

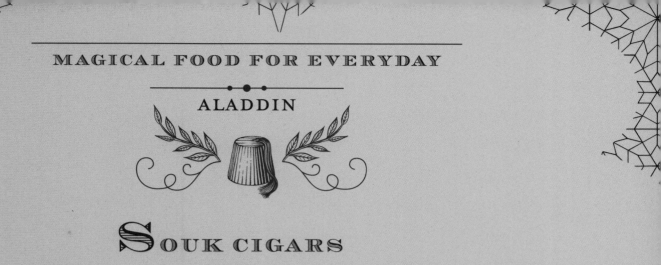

SOUK CIGARS

Welcome, noble stranger, your presence honors one of the most esteemed souks in Arabia! Inhale these incomparable incenses and perfumes, marvel at the fine quality of these fabrics! What was that? You seek something even more precious? Some sort of remarkable lamp? I recognized you, O Great Wizard! Let me find it for you! I insist! And while you wait, sit and enjoy the best cigars of the souk, the pride of our lands!

PREPARATION TIME • 20 mins ◆ COOKING TIME • 35 mins

INGREDIENTS
• makes about 20 cigars

2 1/4 lb spinach, fresh if possible

3 1/2 oz sheep's milk cheese (such as feta)

Salt and pepper

10 sheets phyllo dough

8 fl oz (1 cup) milk

1 small cup olive oil

1 3/4 oz sesame seeds

1 small tub plain yogurt

1 squeeze lemon juice

◆ Rinse the spinach thoroughly to rid it of any dust from the souk (remove the larger stems if necessary), then simmer for 20 minutes in salted water. Using a slotted spoon take it out and drop it straight into a large bowl of iced water—that will wake it up!

◆ Drain and chop the spinach, crumble in the cheese, and mix. Above all, Noble Friend, do not forget to season with salt and pepper.

◆ Next, brush a sheet of phyllo dough with milk using a kitchen brush (yes, a brush, even if the carpet insists that you use its tassels).

◆ The next step demands the dexterity of 40 thieves: place a spoonful of mixture 3/4 inch from the bottom of the sheet of phyllo, leaving the necessary space on each side. Fold the pastry over the filling, brush with milk, then fold the sides inward: Ta-da! You have a rectangle!

◆ Preheat the oven to 400°F. Roll the filled part toward the top, remembering to brush the pastry with milk with each turn. Finish all the cigars. What was that? Distracted by the marvels of the souk, you forgot to preheat the oven? Is that a formal wish? It is? In that case, consider it done: here, before you, O my Master, is a perfectly prepared oven. All you have to do now is slide the cigars, brushed with olive oil and sprinkled with delicious sesame seeds, into the oven and wait for about 35 minutes. Be patient, your cigars will be golden and crisp! Enjoy them with yogurt enhanced with a squeeze of lemon juice. Good, no?

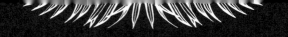

BROCHETTES OF FINELY CHOPPED ENEMY

"When, like me, you are a powerful wizard with designs upon the Sultan's throne, you have to be able to command respect. I'll tell you a secret: ever since my faithful servant spread the rumor that this recipe is made from the flesh of my enemies, they are terrified whenever they see me. Ha! ha! ha!" —The Vizier

PREPARATION TIME • 5 mins ◆ COOKING TIME • 20 mins

SOAKING TIME • 1 night ◆ RESTING TIME • 30 mins

◆ Remember to soak your chickpeas in water. There's nothing like a good night's sleep to soften them up.

◆ The next day, drain the chickpeas, wrap them in a dish towel, and rub them vigorously to remove their skin. Crush them mercilessly, then reduce them to a purée.

◆ Finely chop the onion, crush the garlic, rinse the parsley and the cilantro and delicately shred them.

◆ Mix together the herbs, cumin, puréed enemy . . . I beg your pardon, the puréed chickpeas, add 3 cups water and the baking powder, and mix again to make sure any insubordinate ingredients know who's in charge! Taste, season with salt and pepper, and leave them to rest and reflect for 30 minutes.

◆ Heat some oil in a large saucepan or deep fryer to 350°F.

◆ After 30 minutes, shape small balls of mixture with a spoon and cook them in the oil until they are golden brown. Impale them on skewers, drizzle with lemon juice, and enjoy with a simple seasonal salad while dreaming up your next Machiavellian plan.

INGREDIENTS • serves 6

1 lb 2 oz chickpeas
1 onion
2 garlic cloves
2 t flat-leaf (Italian) parsley leaves
1 t cilantro leaves
1 t cumin
1 t baking powder
Salt and pepper
Oil for deep frying
Juice of 1 lemon
1 seasonal lettuce

ALADDIN

Morsels from the Cave of Wonders

"Salaam, Esteemed Effendi, who rubbed my lamp . . . allow your humble servant to introduce you to these sweetmeats straight from the Cave of Wonders." —The Genie of the Lamp

PREPARATION TIME • 20 mins   ◆   COOKING TIME • 50 mins

INGREDIENTS • serves 4

1 lb 2 oz carrots

8 fl oz (1 cup) milk

3 1/2 oz superfine sugar

1 oz currants (dry)

4 cardamom pods

1 oz unsalted pistachios

1 3/4 oz butter

1 oz flaked and toasted almonds

◆ To sample these squares, my Friend, you must wash, peel, and finely grate the carrots.

◆ Then, put them in a saucepan over high heat—watch your fingers!—and add the milk and enough water to cover the carrots. Next, ask the carpet to add the sugar and mix gently until it is dissolved (the sugar, not the carpet). Lower the heat and let it simmer for the time it takes to admire the sun setting over the desert (about 45 minutes).

◆ As the last rays are fading, soak the currants in a little lukewarm water.

◆ Remove the cardamom seeds from their pods and grind them to a powder by asking an elephant to stamp on them. If you don't have an elephant, you can also take two spoons and crush the seeds by pressing them against each other—or else use a food processor, but it is noisy and not as amusing. But, by my beard, I am forgetting something, the pistachios must also be roughly chopped!

◆ When the sun has disappeared behind the dunes and the carrots have absorbed almost all the milk, add the drained currants, ground cardamom, and chopped pistachios, then add the butter in pieces and leave to cook for 5 minutes, just enough time to grant a wish.

◆ Spoon mixture into a dish or tray and allow it to cool completely before cutting into squares. Scatter with almonds.

◆ Cut into squares and enjoy as you contemplate the moonlight.

Pumpkin soup

To celebrate Halloween, here is a recipe that delights sorcerers both of this world and the next, from that most esteemed authority on the subject of pumpkins: Cinderella's fairy godmother.

INGREDIENTS • serves 4

One 2 1/4 lb winter squash from the garden (red kuri, butternut, Hungarian blue . . .)
1 chicken bouillon cube
Freshly grated nutmeg
Salt and pepper
2 1/4 oz crème fraîche or sour cream

PREPARATION TIME • 30 mins   ◆   COOKING TIME • 45 mins

◆ Fetch your best pumpkin from the bottom of the garden (not the biggest one, you might need that for a coach), brush off the lizard, find your wand (up your sleeve, perhaps?), take a deep breath, smile, and cut the pumpkin into large pieces, carefully. Remove the seeds.

◆ If cooking in a cauldron: don your protective gloves and carefully remove the peel of the pumpkin. Place the pieces in your pot, cover with water and a shower of sparkles, crumble in the bouillon cube, and cook for 45 minutes.

◆ If you are using a steamer: crumble the bouillon cube into a bowl of water to add to the pumpkin later. Place the pumpkin pieces in the steam basket without removing the peel and cook for about 45 minutes, until the flesh is as tender as a fairy's smile and can be easily pierced with the tip of your wand. Let it cool for a few minutes, then remove the peel by gently pulling it off.

◆ Blend the cooked pumpkin pieces in a food processor, adding a little of the cooking liquid until you have a smooth, fluid soup. Taste, ask the mice and the lizard for their opinion, and add grated nutmeg, salt, and pepper to your preference (the opinion of the mice is decidedly too weird).

◆ Pour into bowls, add the crème fraîche or sour cream, and serve. Let your guests enjoy, but only after casting a protective spell over their clothes—it would be a shame to have to change and be late for the ball.

CAIR PARAVEL EGGS

Lucy, Edmund, Susan, and Peter, and not forgetting Caspian . . . over the centuries many have sat at Cair Paravel, the castle where the kings and queens of Narnia hold court. Many remarkable banquets have been held there, but the dish that has been most well-received is based on eggs. Why? Because wherever and whenever you eat it—in the middle of nowhere or in some very tricky situation—it will always be like being at home.

PREPARATION TIME • 5 mins ◆ COOKING TIME • 10 mins

INGREDIENTS • serves 4

1/2 baguette
3 1/2 oz thick-cut bacon, cut into lardons
Sunflower oil
4 eggs
Pepper

◆ When the sun rises over the land of Aslan, cut half a baguette into 4 pieces, 2 inches long, and pull out some of the crumb to make a nest; set aside.

◆ Sauté the bacon for a few minutes in a nonstick frying pan until golden brown, drain off the excess fat, and set aside.

◆ Pour the oil into the frying pan. When it is hot, place the bread nests in the pan, hole-side up.

◆ Break the eggs carefully. Gently slide each egg into a hole, lightly pressing the baguette so the egg white doesn't run underneath the bread. Season with pepper.

◆ Cook for 2 minutes, then turn the nest over with a spatula and cook for another 2 minutes.

◆ When the bread is as golden as the coat of the Great Lion, place it on a plate and scatter over the bacon pieces.

Ramandu's Island Salad

When the crew of the Dawn Treader *arrives on Ramandu's Island, a strange scene greets them: three Narnian lords, heads on their plates, sleeping an enchanted sleep in the middle of a vast banquet. Every evening, great, elegant birds, white as snow, replace the dishes, to the great amazement of Caspian and his friends. Fortunately, Ramandu and his daughter Evening Star explain the reasons for this spell. The huge feast, prepared at the behest of Aslan, honors the warm and pleasant island that marks the beginning of the World's End, so it is natural that the dishes give pride of place to seafood and the foods of the tropics.*

PREPARATION TIME • 15 mins ◆ MARINATING TIME • 5 hrs

DISGORGING TIME • 15 mins

INGREDIENTS • serves 4

◆ Place the lemons on the banqueting table and, pressing down on them firmly beneath the palm of your hand, roll each lemon back and forth a few times. Then cut them in half over a bowl and squeeze them to extract all their juice.

◆ Rinse the fish, check that there are no bones left. Using the broad Stone Knife lying on the table, cut the fish into pieces. Place the pieces in a dish, cover with lemon juice, cover the dish with plastic wrap, and marinate in the refrigerator for 5 hours.

◆ When the Evening Star fades, drain the fish.

◆ Peel the cucumber and cut it into cubes. Dust the cubes lightly with salt before placing them in a strainer to disgorge for 15 minutes. Peel the shallot and carrots, then thinly slice the shallot and cut the carrots into sticks. Rinse the tomatoes and chives. Dice the tomatoes and chop the chives.

◆ Gently combine the pieces of fish, cucumber, shallot, carrots, and tomatoes in a mixing bowl. Pour the coconut milk over top, stir again, and sprinkle with chopped chives. Serve immediately.

5 lemons

1 lb 2 oz whiting fillets (bream or cod)

1/2 cucumber

Salt

1 shallot

2 carrots

2 tomatoes

1 bunch chives

3 1/2 oz coconut milk

Soufflé Omelet Saruman

Saruman is a wizard with great power, much of which lies in his mesmerizing voice that enchants many a creature. His ambition led him to succumb to the mirages of Sauron. After the fall of Isengard, Merry and Pippin regain their composure thanks to this omelet made from ingredients they found in the guard room of the White Tower.

INGREDIENTS • serves 4

8 eggs
4 1/2 oz pouring cream
Salt and pepper
1/2 oz butter

PREPARATION TIME • 15 mins ◆ COOKING TIME • 6 to 8 mins

◆ Break your eggs over a bowl, separating the yolks from the whites.

◆ Start a tornado in a bowl (or use a mixer) and beat the whites until firm peaks form.

◆ Pour the cream into a bowl that has been chilled in the freezer, unleash the winds of Caradhras, and beat the cream until it thickens.

◆ In another bowl, break up the yolks with a whisk, add the whipped cream, then the beaten egg whites, and season with salt and pepper.

◆ Heat the butter in a frying pan as hot as a palantír, pour in the mixture, and cook for 3 to 4 minutes until the omelet is set.

◆ Fold the edges toward the center and cook for another 3 or 4 minutes. Serve immediately.

Radagast's salad

Radagast the Brown is a wizard living on the edge of Mirkwood. Also called Aiwendil meaning "friend to birds," he prefers the company of animals and plants to that of men. In the film The Hobbit, *it is Radagast who warns Gandalf about the return of an evil presence in the stronghold of Dol Guldur.*

PREPARATION TIME • 10 mins ◆ COOKING TIME • 45 mins

INGREDIENTS • serves 4

2 raw beets
1 bunch of watercress
9 oz mushrooms
1 handful walnuts
2 T walnut oil
1 T apple cider vinegar
Salt and pepper

◆ Preheat the oven to 350°F.

◆ Rinse the beets and wrap them in parchment paper or a sheet of aluminum foil. Place them in the oven or under the ashes of a good fire, and cook them until a knife pierces them easily (about 45 minutes).

◆ Rinse the watercress leaves well in the clear water of a stream, then spin them dry.

◆ Making sure that all of your mushrooms are indeed safe to eat, brush them and clean with a damp cloth. Slice them very thinly and fry for a few minutes in a frying pan over high heat until they start to brown.

◆ Crack the walnuts and collect the kernels.

◆ Make a vinaigrette by mixing together the oil, vinegar, salt, and pepper.

◆ Peel the beets and cut them into pieces. In a large bowl, combine the pieces of beet, the cooled mushrooms, the watercress, and the walnuts, and add the dressing just before serving.

Beorn's goat cheese toast

In The Hobbit, *when Bilbo and his companions find refuge at Beorn's home after fleeing the orcs, the man–bear treats them to toast with cheese from his goats and honey from Mirkwood.*

INGREDIENTS • serves 4

4 small or 2 large goat cheese logs
Salt and pepper
1 pinch freshly grated nutmeg
4 slices bread
1 handful fresh herbs (basil, marjoram, thyme)
4 T honey
1 seasonal lettuce (batavia, mâche)

PREPARATION TIME • 10 mins ◆ COOKING TIME • 5 mins

◆ Using a very sharp blade, cut each small cheese in half lengthwise, or each large cheese into slices 1/2-inch thick.

◆ Season with salt and pepper, sprinkle lightly with nutmeg, and lay the pieces of cheese on the bread slices.

◆ Pick some herbs growing south of the gate. Rinse, drain, and chop them finely. Sprinkle the slices with fresh herbs and then drizzle with honey.

◆ Place them under a broiler for about 5 minutes, until the cheese melts, the honey caramelizes, and the bread becomes crusty. Serve with seasonal salad.

KEBAB OF 3,000 YEARS AGO

Ah, the splendor of the walls of Ur, of Babylon the magnificent. . . . Only we forget to mention that it was the djinn—well, mostly Bartimaeus—who built these cities that became legendary for their beauty. The only drawback was that he was constantly preparing this dish for Faquarl and Jabor, who would demand a snack each time they finished a section of wall.

PREPARATION TIME • 15 mins ◆ COOKING TIME • 25 mins

RESTING TIME • 45 mins

◆ Mix the flatbread ingredients together, then knead the dough. When it is smooth and not sticky, let it stand for 45 minutes.

◆ In your incarnation as a fire spirit, toast the sesame seeds with a glance (alternatively, toast in a frying pan over medium heat)—they should be golden but not too brown. In a mortar of the purest marble (or a blender), crush the seeds with an equal amount of oil and mash until the mixture is smooth and even.

◆ Finely chop the cilantro. With an elegant gesture, peel the onion and slice it into strips. Soften the strips in a frying pan over medium heat until translucent, then add the meat and cumin and cook for 5 minutes. Add the cilantro, mix, season, with salt and pepper, and let cool.

◆ Divide the dough into 6 equal pieces, and roll them out very thinly on a floured work surface. Lay them in a very hot frying pan and let them cook for 5 to 7 minutes on each side: they should brown lightly and puff up like an exasperated magician.

◆ Open up each flatbread, fill with some of the meat mixture and crumbled cheese, add a generous spoonful of the sesame sauce, and eat hot, admiring the rising waters of the River Jordan.

INGREDIENTS • serves 6

The flatbreads

14 oz flour + extra for work surface
1 t baking powder
1 t superfine sugar
1 t salt
1 1/2 oz butter, melted
8 fl oz (1 cup) milk

The filling

Sesame seeds
Olive oil
1 handful cilantro leaves
1 onion
9 oz leftover meat
1 t cumin
Salt and pepper
3 1/2 oz sheep's milk cheese, crumbled

CUCUMBER SANDWICHES

As the youngest Minister for Information of all time, Nathaniel—who elects to become John Mandrake—is a regular guest at government receptions. Which is just as well, because otherwise how would he prevent an ambitious, powerful, and really very cunning wizard, accompanied by a legion of djinn, from taking advantage of a cocktail party to try to seize power? That said, even at the highest levels, and right in the middle of a battle where golems mingle with magical spells and amulets, the cream of British magicians cannot pass up these famous cucumber sandwiches.

PREPARATION TIME • 20 mins

♦ Peel the cucumber and slice it as thinly as possible; ideally you will have conjured up a djinni with a mandoline or razor-sharp claws. Salt the cucumber slices, place them in a strainer in the sink, and let them drain for 15 minutes, the time it takes to discipline the unruly djinni who is making rude remarks about the addiction of British magicians to cucumber sandwiches.

♦ Find your place again in your recipe and blot the cucumber slices with paper towels.

♦ Toast the slices of bread, then spread them with butter. Arrange the cucumber slices in an attractive pattern on a slice of whole wheat bread, disregarding the disparaging comments of the djinni who says this is pointless because the cucumber will be on the inside of the sandwich. Ignore him, he does not know what he is talking about. If he insists, threaten to enclose him in a bottle for the rest of his summoning—that'll teach him.

♦ Sprinkle the rounds of cucumber with finely chopped mint, cover with a slice of white bread, and press down lightly. Do the same with the other slices of bread. Cut the sandwich into quarters on the diagonal and enjoy while keeping an eye on the megalomaniac wizard who would like to destroy your career.

INGREDIENTS • makes 8 sandwiches or 32 mini-sandwiches

1 cucumber
8 slices whole wheat sandwich bread
8 slices white sandwich bread
3 1/2 oz unsalted butter
2 t freshly chopped mint
Salt and pepper

Babylonian pottage

When the divine Queen of Sheba asks the djinni Bartimaeus to take her magician Asmira across the vast desert to spy on the great King Solomon—hallowed be his slippers—she doesn't think about how her companion will eat. It is always the same with the great and the good, they don't think about logistics and detail! And who saves the day by cooking up a good restoring and comforting soup? Bartimaeus!

PREPARATION TIME • 10 mins • COOKING TIME • 45 mins

- Make the most of the scorching midday sun to toast your lentils in a pan over medium heat. A few minutes is enough; you don't want to burn them.

- Rinse the pieces of chicken by summoning up a spurt of water. While you're at it, rinse the cilantro and the watercress or arugula as well. Peel the onions (and if you start to cry and blow your nose on the flying carpet, do it discreetly, wizards are rather sensitive about this, I don't know why) and cut each of them into four. Wash and cut the leeks.

- Place a large pot on high heat and add the toasted lentils, pieces of chicken, cilantro, watercress or arugula, onion, leek, crushed garlic, and cumin. Add the milk and enough water to cover the mixture. When bubbles appear, reduce the heat and simmer for 45 minutes until the chicken meat comes away from the bone.

- Enjoy hot.

If you can cook this soup on a flying carpet while avoiding marauding desert bandits, there is no reason why it shouldn't work! Okay, maybe there is. Because you aren't an amazing djinni able to view seven planes!

INGREDIENTS • serves 6

- **for 6 Babylonian djinn**
Several pieces of poultry
1 handful beggarweed
2 Samidu
1 Sahumu
1 Suhutinuu
1 handful Sahlu or Engengeru
Kisiburu leaves
1 nib Kamu
1 jug of Kisimmu

- **for 6 modern djinn**
1 handful red lentils
6 chicken pieces on the bone (thighs, wings . . .)
1 bunch cilantro
1 handful watercress or arugula
2 onions
1 leek
1 garlic clove
1 t cumin
2 pt (4 cups) milk

SARDINE SANDWICHES

When he can't stop laughing, Mary Poppins' Uncle Albert floats up to the ceiling, where he rolls about in fits of giggles! Although this behavior is somewhat inappropriate—how are you supposed to drink your tea without spilling it when you're bobbing around high above the floor?—these sandwiches are perfect for teatime with a bird's-eye view!

PREPARATION TIME • 5 mins

Note: Do your best to keep your composure so you don't float away before finishing the sandwiches.

INGREDIENTS • serves 4

9 oz canned sardines in water
1 oz unsalted butter
Juice of 1 lime
Salt and pepper
8 cherry tomatoes
8 slices white sandwich bread

◆ Drain the sardines, cut them in half lengthwise and remove the backbone. Mash them in a bowl with the butter and lime juice, and season with salt and pepper.

◆ Rinse the cherry tomatoes, cut them in half, and let them drain for a few moments. Don't make any jokes or tell any funny stories or hilarious anecdotes; keep a straight face . . . or you will take off and not come back down!

◆ Spread half of the bread slices with the fishy mixture, place a tomato half in the center of each, and top with the second slice of bread.

◆ Tssttssstss, I hear you tittering. . . . Come on, be serious just a little longer! Ignore Uncle Albert, who is bouncing off the walls in time with his uncontrollable laughter, and cut the sandwiches using the cookie cutter of your choice (star, umbrella, parrot). Now that you've reached this point you're nearly there, take a deep breath, arrange the remaining tomato halves on top . . . and now you can at last let out all the laughter. Enjoy on the ceiling!

Peelings soup

One fine morning, when Cedric Brown's seven children were pretending to be sick and refusing to get up, Nanny McPhee glued them to their beds for the whole day. Later, as the sun was setting, she served them this soup. It may be made from humble vegetable peelings but to the hungry children it was the best dish they had ever tasted.

INGREDIENTS • serves 6

2 lb 4 oz vegetable trimmings, as diverse as they are varied (potatoes, carrots, parsnips, radish tops, beets . . .)
1 small handful fresh herbs (thyme, bay leaf, rosemary)
1 chicken bouillon cube
Salt and pepper
1 packet (9 oz) noodles

PREPARATION TIME • 15 mins ◆ COOKING TIME • 45 mins

◆ Rinse the peelings and sort them, discarding any that are bruised or moldy. Set aside a few for garnish. Wash the herbs as well.

◆ Place the peelings in a large pot, crumble in the bouillon cube, add the herbs, season with salt and pepper, and cover with fresh water.

◆ Bring to a boil. When the first bubble bursts, lower the heat and simmer for 45 minutes. Use this time to check that the supposedly sick children are actually lying in their beds rather than using them as trampolines.

◆ Heat a saucepan of water, cook the noodles according to the time indicated on the packet, drain, and set aside.

◆ Preheat the oven to 450°F.

◆ Spread the reserved peelings on a baking sheet and bake for 5 to 10 minutes, depending on their thickness, until they are nice and crispy.

◆ Strain the broth and serve it very hot with the noodles and crisped peelings, after having lifted the spell gluing the children to their beds, of course!

Magical gratin

We modern-day witches and wizards lead a hectic life, especially when we live with humans who are unaware of our existence. That's why sometimes we need to take it easy—or wave our wands—and, like Samantha, Darrin, and Tabitha, enjoy a good, satisfying meal at home as a family. In such cases, you simply can't beat macaroni and cheese.

PREPARATION TIME • 15 mins   ◆   COOKING TIME • 30 mins

INGREDIENTS • serves 6

Oh Daughters of Selene and Residents of Limbo, hear me!
May the oven reach 350°F,
May the onion be peeled without tears and finely chopped,
May the tomatoes be washed and cut into pieces,
May the beef be sautéed for 10 minutes on high heat,
May the macaroni be cooked in five times their volume of boiling water,
then drained,
May the meat and tomatoes, onions and pasta, and salt and pepper be
mixed together in a large dish,
May the butter and two-thirds of the cheese be added before all is again mixed,
May the mixture be divided into as many ramekins as guests,
May the remaining cheese cover all,
And may the ramekins rest in the embers of the oven for 20 minutes!
Oh Residents of Limbo! Oh Daughters of Selene!
May nobody disturb us in this moment,
May this moment be sacred and may we share it in peace!

1 onion
2 1/4 lb tomatoes
1 lb 2 oz ground beef
1 packet (1 lb 2 oz) macaroni
Salt and pepper
9 oz grated Cheddar cheese (try it
as well with Parmesan, Mimolette,
or Gruyère)
1 3/4 oz butter

Witches' Soup

Although simple to make, this appetizer is a favorite of all the witches, including the Grand High Witch, when they get together for their great Annual Meeting. . . . Unless, of course, they first swallow the Delayed Action Formula 86 and find themselves turning into mice. But you don't need to wait for an Annual Meeting, you can try this recipe yourself at home.

INGREDIENTS • serves 4

16 fl oz (2 cups) tomato juice
2 1/4 oz tapioca pearls
4 potatoes
2 1/4 lb zucchini
Salt and pepper

PREPARATION TIME • 15 mins • COOKING TIME • 1 hr 10 mins

◆ Bring the tomato juice to a boil and cook the tapioca in it verrry gently for tventy minutes.

◆ Rrrinse and peel the potatoes, and cut them into verrry large pieces.

◆ Rrrepeat with the zucchini.

◆ Place the pieces of potato in a larrrge saucepan of boiling vater. Let them cook for 30 minutes, after vich you add the zucchini and simmerrr for another tventy minutes.

◆ Now drain the tapioca pearrrls (keep the tomato juice to use in another potion).

◆ Rrremove the saucepan from the heat and blend, grrrind, crrrush, and pulverrrize yourr soup in a powerrrful food processorrr until it is completely combined.

◆ Taste, add salt and pepperrr, then add the verrry rrred tapioca to your verrry grrreen soup and eat verrry hot.

RED DRAGON INN FIERY BROTH

The Red Dragon Inn is near the coast, whose high cliffs are home to a vast colony of dragons. All the paladins, rogues, mages, and druids who have tried it are of the same mind: it is best to think twice before picking a quarrel with a dragon in its lair. A look of sympathy passes between them, when one relates how things got a little too close for comfort. That's why the inn's jolly cook has created this recipe that is both sweet and fiery. Everyone agrees that in addition to being delicious and comforting, his soup is also ideal for exploring forgotten underground passages or facing a night full of darkness and terror.

PREPARATION TIME • 10 mins ◆ COOKING TIME • 45 mins

INGREDIENTS • serves 4

1 onion

3 garlic cloves

2 celery stalks

1/2 oz fresh ginger root

1 3/4 oz coconut milk

2 pt (4 cups) chicken broth

1 small tin tomato paste

1 T curry powder

4 cornichons (baby pickled cucumbers)

Salt and pepper

Tabasco sauce, to taste

◆ Peel the onion, garlic, celery, and ginger. Cut them into large pieces and put them in a saucepan, to which you will add the coconut milk, chicken broth, tomato paste, curry powder, and cornichons.

◆ Mix together well and bring to a boil. Simmer and reduce for about 45 minutes. Taste and season.

◆ Strain the soup through a strainer, then through a cloth to obtain a very clear broth. Taste, adjust the seasoning if necessary, and add Tabasco sauce to taste.

◆ Serve steaming hot.

NAGRAND TEMPURA

Climb on the back of your griffin or wolf and set out for Nagrand! An Outland zone located on what was once Draenor, Nagrand is the most beautiful landscape in World of Warcraft. Fertile soil, verdant hills coupled with waterfalls cascading between rocky peaks. . . . If you can evade the many clans and wild beasts, there's nothing to stop you from taking a break there and enjoying the famous Nagrand tempura to restore your vitality and mana!

PREPARATION TIME • 45 mins   •   COOKING TIME • 5 mins

INGREDIENTS • serves 4

◆ Whisk the egg and iced water together in the skull of an orc, or a bowl. Add the flour little by little, the paprika and salt, and then the ice cube.

◆ Peel the shrimp.

◆ Peel the vegetables. Slice the carrots and zucchini very thinly; separate the broccoli florets.

◆ Heat some salted water until boiling in a cauldron. Throw in your vegetables, and leave them for 1 minute, or the time it takes to recite a spell and provoke the wrath of Archimonde. Drain and dry well with paper towels.

◆ Heat some oil in a large saucepan or deep fryer to 350°F.

◆ Spellbind the shrimp and vegetables by dipping them in the batter, then fry them in the oil for 1 minute. Remove them from the oil and place on paper towels or the dried skin of a cloven-footed creature, if you have some on hand, then season with salt.

◆ Vigorously whisk the apricot jam and olive oil together in a bowl and add the Espelette pepper. Serve the tempura straight away with the sauce on the side.

The batter

1 egg
5 fl oz (2/3 cup) iced water
3 1/2 oz flour
1 t paprika
Salt
1 ice cube
Oil for deep frying

The main foods

8 large shrimp
2 carrots
1 zucchini
7 oz broccoli

The sauce

1 T apricot jam
3½ fl oz olive oil
2 pinches Espelette pepper (mild chili powder)

Pasta from the lair of Magica de Spell

When she is not busy trying to steal Scrooge's lucky dime, Magica lives on the slopes of Vesuvius. Here is a typical recipe from her lair, providing the energy she needs to work out her dark schemes.

INGREDIENTS • serves 4

2 lb 4 oz mussels
1 packet (1 lb 2 oz) spaghetti
Olive oil
2 garlic cloves
1/2 fish bouillon cube
9 oz ripe tomatoes, ready to use
Salt and pepper
1 T chopped fresh parsley

PREPARATION TIME • 20 mins ◆ COOKING TIME • 15 mins

◆ Clean the mussels: remove any with broken or open shells, then scrape the rest to remove any threads and traces of shell.

◆ Wash the mussels in a large quantity of water to rid them of sand. Finally, plunge them into a basin of cold water and ruthlessly eliminate any that float.

◆ Cook the spaghetti in a large cauldron of boiling salted water according to box or package directions, drain, and rinse so it doesn't stick together. Set aside.

◆ Heat some olive oil in a second cauldron over low heat.

◆ Peel the garlic, cut it into pieces, and throw them into the cauldron with the mussels, 1/2 cup water, and the fish bouillon cube. Bring to a simmer for five minutes.

◆ Ruthlessly eliminate any mussels that aren't open. Strain and reserve the juices and remove the mussels from their shells.

◆ Rinse the tomatoes and dice them finely.

◆ Return the cooking juices to the cauldron, add the tomatoes, mussels, and spaghetti, season with salt and pepper, and heat through for 2 minutes before serving steaming hot sprinkled with the freshly chopped parsley.

CHICKEN WITH CHERRIES FROM THE COLD LANDS

In Hans Christian Andersen's fairy tale, when Gerda goes in search of Kai, who has been kidnapped by the Snow Queen, she arrives at a curious cottage. The old woman who lives there insists that she stay and lets her eat as many of the cherries that grow in her orchard as Gerda likes. There are indeed cherries in Denmark, and they are even the central feature of this traditional dish!

INGREDIENTS • serves 4

4 chicken leg quarters
2 3/4 oz butter
8 fl oz (1 cup) cherry juice
2 T orange juice
1 T honey
2 T red currant jelly
2 1/4 lb potatoes
Juice of 1 lemon
9 oz pitted cherries
Salt and pepper

PREPARATION TIME • 15 mins ◆ COOKING TIME • 50 mins

◆ In a flameproof casserole dish over high heat, panfry the chicken pieces with half the butter until well-browned on all sides, then add the cherry juice, orange juice, honey, and red currant jelly. Simmer for 25 minutes, spooning the liquid over the chicken at regular intervals.

◆ Meanwhile, wash and peel the potatoes, then steam them or boil them in salted boiling water for about 25 minutes, until the tip of a sharp knife easily pierces their hearts.

◆ Remove the chicken from the flameproof casserole dish and set it aside.

◆ Strain and reserve the sauce and deglaze the casserole dish with the lemon juice, scraping up all the browned bits from the base of the pot. Add the rest of the butter, the chicken, the strained sauce, and the cherries, and cook for another 5 minutes, just long enough to heat through. Season with salt and pepper.

◆ Serve piping hot with the steamed potatoes.

Scarecrow bread

When you are a scarecrow who is a lot smarter than people think, it's a good idea to make a mental note of all the recipes evoked by the farmer. It can turn out to be very useful when you are lost and wandering in the middle of a strange world, with just a few ears of corn up your sleeve and a girl called Dorothy who is as hungry as she is charming.

PREPARATION TIME • 5 mins ◆ COOKING TIME • 35 mins

◆ Preheat the oven to 400°F.

◆ Sift the cornmeal, cornstarch, baking powder, and salt into a large mixing bowl. Add the egg and the oil, and blend with the milk.

◆ If, along the way, you happen to have met a local with a well-stocked pantry, add the following ingredients: ground meat, vinegar, pepper, mustard, Worcestershire sauce, and pickled peppers, cut into strips. Mix until the batter is smooth.

◆ Pour into a loaf pan and bake for 35 minutes. Cool a little before serving.

INGREDIENTS • makes 1 loaf

9 oz cornmeal
9 oz cornstarch
1 t baking powder
1 pinch salt
1 egg
4 T sunflower oil
8 fl oz (1 cup) milk

Optional

7 oz ground meat
4 T cider vinegar
4 T pepper
4 T mustard
4 T Worcestershire sauce
1 jar of pickled peppers

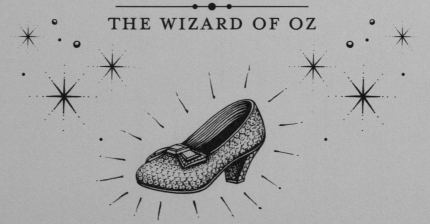

Dorothy's toast

Made with Aunt Em's jams and Uncle Henry's goat's milk, Dorothy's toasts keep her and her dog Toto going until they meet the Tin Man, the Lion, and Scarecrow.

PREPARATION TIME • 5 mins

INGREDIENTS • 8 toasts

1 sprig rosemary
1 log goat cheese
(Sainte-Maure style)
1 jar apricot jam
8 slices pain d'épice (French spice bread)

◆ Rinse the rosemary, remove the leaves from the stem, and chop finely. Remove any straw from around the log of goat cheese, kindly provided by Uncle Henry's goat, then cut into slices about 1/8-inch thick.

◆ Spread the apricot jam on the slices of pain d'épice, then lay a slice of cheese on top (or more depending on the size of the bread and your appetite) and sprinkle with rosemary leaves.

The Ancient One's Tibetan Momo

On his journey to Tibet, where he hopes to find a miracle cure, Steven Strange encounters the Ancient One, a man with unusual powers. After a difficult initiation process, Strange realizes his past mistakes and that he now, too, has certain powers. When undergoing trials of sorcery, there's nothing quite like this traditional Tibetan dish taken with your mystical master!

PREPARATION TIME • 45 mins ◆ COOKING TIME • 15 mins

RESTING TIME • 20 mins

◆ Take your place in the kitchen of the Ancient One and find a bowl. Pour 10 fl oz (1 1/4 cups) of water and the salt into it.

◆ Using your new powers (or a whisk), swirl the water and gradually mix in the flour. Knead the dough for 5 minutes and let it rest, covered with plastic wrap, for 20 minutes.

◆ Shred the Chinese cabbage with a saber or a sharp knife. Peel and chop the garlic after removing the sprout from the middle. Peel and finely chop the shallot. Wash and chop the cilantro leaves.

◆ Mix the ground beef with the rest of the filling ingredients in a bowl. Season with salt and pepper according to your mystical tastes.

◆ Shape the dough into small balls.

◆ Roll out the dough flat on a floured surface and cut out 4 circles with a cookie cutter. Place a little filling in the middle of each circle and fold the edges over to close it up. Lightly moisten the edges with your finger to make them easier to seal.

◆ Bake for 15 minutes in a steamer or in a pot on a rack that sits above the surface of the water. Serve immediately.

INGREDIENTS • serves 4

The pastry
1 lb 2 oz flour + extra for work surface
1 t salt

The filling
5 1/2 oz Chinese cabbage
1 garlic clove
1 shallot
3 sprigs cilantro
14 oz ground beef
2 T soy sauce
1 T ginger
Salt and pepper

FEASTS FOR SPECIAL DAYS

Rafiki's chips

A traditional dish of the Pride Lands, perfect for preparing the spoils of the hunt, Rafiki, the monkey shaman of the Lion kings, would always be ready to try some.

INGREDIENTS • serves 4

1 lb 2 oz wildebeest meat
(or rump steak)
1 T pink flamingo (or duck) fat
4 T umbrella tree essence (or sweet
soy sauce)
4 T date palm spirit (or wine
vinegar)
2 T honey
4 T coffee
2 T barbecue spice mix

PREPARATION TIME • 10 mins ◆ COOKING TIME • 4 hrs

FREEZING TIME • 45 mins ◆ RESTING TIME • 1 night

◆ The shaman stores the piece of wildebeest that the Great Lion has granted him for 45 minutes in the coldest place he can find so it will be easier to carve.

◆ Meanwhile, he melts the fat in a pot over low heat, adds the umbrella tree essence, the date palm spirit, honey, and 2 tablespoons of water.

◆ Summoning the spirit of the savanna, he boils everything for the time it takes a warthog to shake off a hyena (about 5 minutes of human time).

◆ After removing the pot from the heat source, he adds the coffee and spice mix, and lets cool in a cave hidden behind a waterfall.

◆ Now the monkey shaman asks one of the Lords of the Plain to use its sharp claws to carve the meat along the grain into thin strips. He pours the sauce into a dish, adds the meat strips, and lets it marinate in the refrigerator overnight.

◆ The next day he drains the meat and threads the strips on acacia wood skewers (be sure to find some that can withstand high heat!). The shaman places these on the highest oven rack, with the drip pan on the lowest. He can then prop the oven door slightly ajar. He dries the meat this way for at least 4 hours in an oven preheated at 150°F.

◆ Rafiki's chips can be stored in a dry place and eaten during the dry season when the herds have disappeared along with the rains.

Newt Scamander's Sasquatch Bait

In the textbook on fantastic beasts that he wrote after leaving Hogwarts, Newt Scamander explains that the Sasquatch is a particularly shy creature, but is very fond of mushrooms—especially the wood blewit. Place some of these mushrooms in a prominent position at the northwest corner of an intersection of two paths, and you will stand a much better chance of attracting one. And if you make this dish . . . they are bound to succumb.

PREPARATION TIME • 10 mins ◆ COOKING TIME • 10 mins

- Preheat the oven to 350°F. Check that all the mushrooms are safe to eat and trim the dirty end of the stem.

- Brush the rest of the stem and the caps using a soft brush (or an old toothbrush), then wipe them with a damp cloth. Separate the stems from the caps.

- Peel the shallot and chop it finely with the mushroom stems. Mix the chopped shallot and mushroom stems with the rillettes, taste, season with salt and pepper if needed, and fill each cap with this mixture.

- Bake in the oven for 10 minutes, filled-side up. Sprinkle with chopped parsley and serve hot.

INGREDIENTS • serves 4

8 large mushrooms
1 shallot
3 1/2 oz rillettes
Salt and pepper
1 T chopped fresh parsley

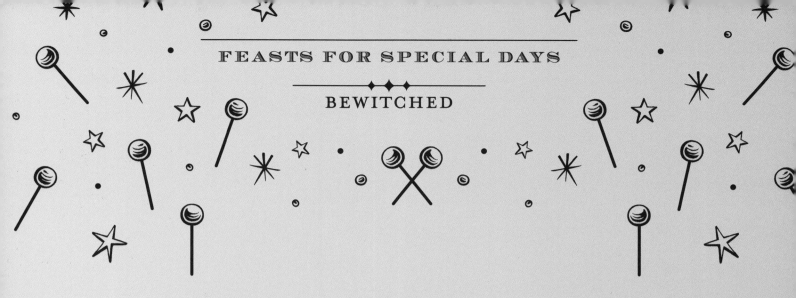

Tabitha's Lollipops

Darrin and Samantha's daughter Tabitha loves these lollipops so much she often makes them levitate toward her from the kitchen, which is a problem when Mrs. Kravitz, a neighbor, is lurking nearby.

INGREDIENTS • serves 6

3 1/2 oz walnuts
3 large cooked beets
(or 4 medium-sized beets)
1 log fresh goat cheese
1 T orange juice
Salt and pepper

PREPARATION TIME • 15 mins

◆ Discreetly, so as not to attract the attention of Mrs. Kravitz, who is pretending to trim the hedge, coarsely chop the nuts.

◆ Peel the beets and cut into cylinders using your special powers, a cylindrical cookie cutter, or a cutter for modeling dough. If you own none of these, cut a wide strip of stiff card, roll it into a cylinder 2 inches in diameter, and use it to make cylinders of beet.

◆ Hollow out the cylinders using a small spoon (or a melon baller) and set aside.

◆ Mash the goat cheese, chop the walnuts, and mix together. Add a little orange juice to loosen the mixture, and season with salt and pepper.

◆ Fill the beet tubes with this mixture, then cut them into slices 1/8–1/4-inch thick. Insert lollipop sticks and serve before Mrs. Kravitz falls off her ladder.

Canapés Endora

Who hasn't dreamed of a Polynesian paradise? In the 1960s, canned pineapple was the key ingredient to give festive dinners a little Hawaiian flavor. The Stephens family joined in the trend: Endora, Samantha's mother, adored these canapés, Uncle Arthur and Aunt Clara took to them in a flash, and Tabitha couldn't get enough of them. Don't lose this recipe—it is still enjoyed by witches of all generations!

INGREDIENTS • serves 6

1 can pineapple in water
(or syrup)
3 slices smoked ham
6 slices whole wheat bread
6 thin slices emmental cheese
1 jar maraschino cherries

PREPARATION TIME • 5 mins ◆ COOKING TIME • 2 mins

◆ If your companions are exclusively witches and wizards, there's no need to use your hands: twitch the tip of your nose, and voila!

◆ Drain the pineapple; remove the rind of the ham.

◆ Place the ingredients on each slice of bread in this order: cheese, ham, and pineapple.

◆ Cut each canapé into quarters and place them briefly under the broiler, just until the cheese melts and the pineapple caramelizes.

◆ Place a maraschino cherry on top of each and serve.

BEWITCHING SCEPTERS

While Mandrake and other modern magicians rarely use a scepter, it is nonetheless a powerful magical object and, as such, highly respected within the magical community. Make these edible scepters to accompany drinks at your next cocktail party for informed wizards.

INGREDIENTS • serves 4

1 lb 2 oz cherry tomatoes, different colors
1 ball (4 1/2 oz) mozzarella cheese
1 T fresh thyme leaves (lemon thyme, if possible)
Pepper from the mill (or somewhere else)
1 packet thin breadsticks

PREPARATION TIME • 10 mins ♦ COOKING TIME • 5 mins

♦ Rinse the tomatoes under a clear stream of water, then dry them with care (and a clean cloth).

♦ Cut the mozzarella into cubes and place in a small cauldron, gently stirring over low heat until the cheese is completely melted.

♦ Add the thyme leaves, season with pepper (don't add salt; the cheese is already salty). Skewer a tomato on a breadstick, then dip the tomatoes in the melted mozzarella and lift gently.

♦ Wrap the stretchy cheese around the breadstick and let the scepters cool, placed stems-down in an (empty) glass. Serve with caution and be on your guard—these scepters are very powerful!

VICE VERSA APPLES

Never trust appearances; the least of things can conceal a surprise or even a trap, as Bartimaeus knows well. These sandwiches will remind you that all may not be as it seems. That strange creature over there, is it human or is it actually a golem ready to do its master's bidding? And that curious amulet hanging from a chain on the chest of the new Minister? And these apples, at first glance so sweet and inoffensive, what are they concealing?

PREPARATION TIME • 10 mins

◆ Peel the apples, remove the cores, and cut them into slices about 1/8-inch thick. Place the slices in lemon juice as you go so they don't oxidize.

◆ Cut the brie into very thin slices. Remove the rind of the ham, then cut out circles from it using a glass as a cookie cutter.

◆ Drain the apples, dry them with paper towels (or a suitable spell), and cut out circles from them using the glass cookie cutter.

◆ Spread ¼ teaspoon of mustard on half of the apple circles, place a slice of brie and a slice of smoked ham on top, and then top with a second apple circle and press down gently. If you're worried about keeping everything in place and don't have a suitable spell to hand, feel free to insert toothpicks through the center.

INGREDIENTS
• makes about 20 sandwiches

4 Granny Smith apples
Juice of 2 lemons
9 oz Brie-type cheese
4 slices York (smoked) ham
4 T whole-grain mustard

HIPPOGRIFF EN PAPILLOTE

Hippogriffs are powerful and very intelligent creatures who are half-eagle, half-horse. Immensely proud, they cannot be enslaved and choose whether to tolerate the company of wizards or not. This earns them the fierce hatred of black magicians, who have no qualms about turning them into a festive dish. . . . That is, if they can manage to catch them!

INGREDIENTS • serves 4

2 3/4 oz butter
14 1/2 oz freshly executed hippogriff
(or 14 oz ostrich meat, cut in pieces)
10 1/2 oz black trumpet mushrooms
1 onion
Salt and pepper
2 1/4 oz red currant jelly
14 oz Vitelotte (purple) potatoes
3 1/2 oz crème fraîche or sour cream

PREPARATION TIME • 30 mins ◆ COOKING TIME • 45 mins

◆ On a very dark night, preheat the oven to 350°F, then add a little of the butter to a pot and quickly sauté the pieces of hippogriff over very high heat so they are browned on all sides. Note: Save a little butter for step 4.

◆ Brush the black trumpet mushrooms to remove any traces of soil, then wipe with a damp cloth.

◆ Peel the onion without crying or whining, and cut it into strips.

◆ When shreds of dark mist start to wrap themselves around your feet, lay out several large sheets of parchment paper and arrange a few pieces of hippogriff on each of them with some mushrooms and onions. Season with salt and pepper, add a knob of butter, and don't forget the red currant jelly.

◆ Ignore the screams that are beginning to rise on this Samhain night, and seal the parcels by folding them on themselves like an accordion, so that all of the lovely aromas are locked in. Bake in the oven for 45 minutes.

◆ While the hippogriff is cooking, wash, peel, and cut up the potatoes. Cook for 40 minutes in a large pot of boiling water until a knife easily pierces their flesh. Mash the potatoes and add the crème fraîche or sour cream.

◆ Serve the hippogriff with the black trumpet mushrooms, the purple mash, and the blood-red sauce.

HARRY POTTER

Little steak and kidney pies

Throughout all of his adventures and years at the Hogwarts School of Witchcraft and Wizardry, Harry particularly relished these pies made with care by the house–elves in the Hogwarts kitchens.

PREPARATION TIME • 30 mins   ◆   COOKING TIME • 1 hr 45 mins

INGREDIENTS • serves 6

1 beef kidney (or diced
or ground beef)

1 lb 10 oz steak

1 oz flour (or cornstarch)

4 1/2 oz forbidden forest
mushrooms

Juice of 1 lemon

2 T oil

1 oz butter

1 onion

2 T Worcestershire sauce

1 T tomato paste

4 fl oz (1/2 cup) dark beer (alcohol-
free)

8 fl oz (1 cup) beef broth

1 t thyme leaves

1 bay leaf

6 oz puff pastry

7 oz shortcrust pastry

1 egg yolk

◆ Remove the kidney membrane with a Disrobing spell, cut the kidney into 8 pieces, and remove any sinew and fat.

◆ Cut the steak into small cubes. Put the flour in a freezer bag, add the steak and kidney, close the bag, and shake to coat the pieces.

◆ After checking that your mushrooms are safe to eat (and that none of them will bite back), clean and trim them, slice them thinly, and pour the lemon juice over them so they don't discolor.

◆ Heat the oil and butter in a heavy-based cauldron or pan. Protect yourself from any tears with a Dry-eye spell, then peel and chop the onion. Soften it in the cauldron for 5 minutes on high heat. Remove the onion and place to one side momentarily. Add the beef and kidney to the pan and cook over high heat for a few minutes until browned on all sides. Replace the onion, and add the Worcestershire sauce, tomato paste, beer, broth, mushrooms, thyme, and bay leaf. Bring to a boil then simmer for 1 hour. Remove the bay leaf.

◆ Preheat the oven to 350°F. Roll out the two pastries. Line 6 small pie pans with the shortcrust pastry to the edge, then add the filling. Cut out lids in the puff pastry, making sure they are 1/2-inch wider than the diameter of the pie pans.

◆ Make a hole in the center of the lids so that the steam can escape. Place them over the filling and seal the edges by pressing them together lightly (or casting a Stick-all spell). Brush with beaten egg yolk and bake in the oven for 45 minutes.

SOUP WITH THE GAZE OF LORD VOLDEMORT'S BASILISK

The Basilisk, a gigantic serpent with sharp and venomous fangs, has a murderous gaze that petrifies whoever meets its eyes. During Harry's second year at Hogwarts, it is a Basilisk introduced by Lord Voldemort that spreads terror throughout the school.

PREPARATION TIME • 10 mins ◆ COOKING TIME • 45 mins

◆ We, obedient Servants of the Master, rinse the watercress and break its stems.

◆ We then wash, peel, and slice the potatoes.

◆ Next, we draw 2 pints (4 cups) of water and heat it over very high heat in a large cauldron. When large bubbles appear, we add the potato slices and let them cook for 35 to 40 minutes, until the tip of a large knife easily penetrates their flesh.

◆ We add the watercress and continue cooking for 5 minutes, before blending in a food processor. We, Servants of the Master, know that the soup with the gaze of the Basilisk should be as green as the scales of the King of Serpents.

◆ Meanwhile, we shall cook the eggs for precisely 9 minutes in boiling water. We will plunge them immediately into iced water to crack their shell and we will cut them carefully to take out the nice round whole yolks. We know that the Master pays particular attention to this detail!

◆ We then cut a slice off one side of each egg yolk so it stays still when it is placed on the plate, and slice the olive into thin narrow strips.

◆ Once the egg yolk has been placed in the middle of a deep plate, we pour in the soup to reach halfway up the side of the plate and place a strip of olive on top of each yolk to form the pupil of the basilisk's terrible yellow eye. We, your Servants, then hasten to serve.

INGREDIENTS • serves 4

1 large bunch watercress (or, if out of season, a mixture of lettuces)
2 medium potatoes
2 pt (4 cups) water
4 eggs
1 black olive

Dufflepud island croquettes

Never risk provoking the wrath of a magician or you could find yourself under a spell and having to wait quite some time before someone comes along to break it. This is what happened to the Dufflepuds (the inhabitants of one of the islands of Narnia): tired of hearing their perpetual whining, a resident magician allowed them to use his magic. They turned into . . . I dare not say. . . . Anyhow, it is better to make friends with sorcerers, and they will turn your meals into feasts. Like the one that was served on this distant island set in warm seas to Caspian, Edmund, Lucy, and Eustace, and which inspired this recipe.

PREPARATION TIME • 10 mins ◆ COOKING TIME • 10 mins

RESTING TIME • 1 hr

INGREDIENTS • serves 4

1 lb 2 oz crab
3 1/2 oz breadcrumbs
1 egg
2 T fromage blanc
1 T whole-grain mustard
1 t Worcestershire sauce
Salt and pepper
1 avocado
1 lemon
Neutral-flavored oil (grapeseed, sunflower . . .)

◆ Shell the crab, making sure to remove any pieces of shell and cartilage, drain it if necessary, and set aside in a covered bowl.

◆ In a bowl, mix the breadcrumbs with the egg, fromage blanc, mustard, and Worcestershire sauce. Taste and season with salt and pepper.

◆ Add the crabmeat, mix together, and shape the mixture into 8 croquettes. Cover with plastic wrap, and let them rest them for 1 hour in the refrigerator.

◆ Peel the avocado and remove the seed. Halve the lemon, slice the avocado, and squeeze over the lemon juice so the avocado doesn't discolor.

◆ Heat 1 tablespoon of the oil in a nonstick frying pan, then fry the croquettes for about 3 to 5 minutes on each side, depending on their size. Serve with the avocado and a squeeze of lemon juice.

CHILDREN EN CROÛTE

In The Silver Chair, *the fourth of the Narnia novels, the giants of Harfang Castle particularly enjoy children en croûte, a dish traditionally served during the Fall Feast. In the absence of any obliging infants, however, you can use veal.*

PREPARATION TIME • 15 mins   ◆   COOKING TIME • 45 mins

INGREDIENTS • serves 6 to 9 giants

◆ Preheat the oven to 350°F.

◆ Sear the veal roast in oil on all sides in a very hot frying pan, then let it rest.

◆ Rinse the basil leaves, dry them with a clean dish towel and, while you're at it, you might like to dry last night's crockery as well.

◆ Using a sharp knife, cut the mozzarella—not your fingers!—into 1/4-inch slices.

◆ Grab a large rolling pin, flatten the puff pastry on your work surface as you would an enemy, and roll it out to a large circle 1/8-inch thick.

◆ The next step is crucial—focus! Three-quarters of an inch inside one edge of the pastry, place a row of Parma ham slices across the middle of the pastry to 3/4 inch inside the opposite edge. Place the slices of mozzarella on top, then the dried tomatoes and basil. It all needs to form a neat, regular row—not be higgledy-piggledy like a bunch of slovenly mountain giants.

◆ Season with pepper—atchoo!—but do not add salt. Lay the roast on your beautiful neat row. Lightly moisten the edges of the pastry and fold the bottom and top over the veal, then fold over the sides. Press down gently on the pastry so the roast is snugly wrapped. Turn it over, dip a brush in the milk and brush all over.

◆ Make two holes in the pastry on top and at each end so that the steam can escape. Bake for 45 minutes before the king and queen of the mountain giants are ready to dine.

1 veal roast, 1 lb 10 oz
Olive oil
6 basil leaves
3 1/2 oz buffalo mozzarella
9 oz puff pastry (from your bakery/ cake shop)
6 slices Parma ham
6 sun-dried tomatoes
Pepper
1 glass milk

DAWN TREADER SOUP

When Caspian, King of Narnia, in the company of Reepicheep the mouse knight, Lucy, Edmund, and Eustace, decides to go in search of the lost Lords of Narnia, he sets sail on a ship called the Dawn Treader. The crew experiences many adventures at sea and on land, and have to live off the food on board and what they can find around them. This soup was a particular favorite of Eustace. . . . At least, until he turned into a dragon! This recipe can easily be made on board a ship, using produce from the sea and supplies from the hold.

PREPARATION TIME • 15 mins ◆ COOKING TIME • 25 mins

INGREDIENTS • serves 4

1 lb 2 oz clams

2 3/4 oz smoked bacon

1 shallot

1 1/2 oz butter

3 sprigs thyme

1 bay leaf

1 T flour

2 cooked potatoes, chopped into chunks

1 3/4 oz crème fraîche or sour cream

Salt and pepper

◆ Collect the clams on the island of Felimath, rinse them carefully, and place in a cauldron with about 4 oz of water. Boil them for 2 minutes, until the clams open, and discard any that remain closed. Drain the clams, saving the juices, and remove them from their shells. Strain and reserve the juices through a piece of cheesecloth.

◆ Chop the bacon and let it brown for a few minutes in a nonstick frying pan. Drain off the excess fat and set the bacon aside on paper towels. Peel the shallot, sauté it for 5 minutes in the butter without browning, then add the bacon, thyme, and bay leaf before the ship reaches the Dark Island.

◆ Sprinkle with the flour and let the shallot and bacon cook for 1 minute, stirring constantly. Slowly add the clam juice, stirring at the same time to prevent lumps forming, then add the potato chunks and simmer for 10 minutes. Remove bay leaf and purée with a blender until the soup is quite smooth. Add the clams and the crème fraîche or sour cream, reheat for 2 minutes, season with salt and pepper, and serve.

Note: Reepicheep likes to add a handful of samphire to nibble with this soup.

Swamp Blob

The swamps. . . . Those dark, damp places that murmur with mysterious sounds and strange animals, giving us . . . goosebumps! Will you have the stomach to sample some Swamp Blob? Who knows what is hiding inside—or what it might have swallowed—before ending up on your plate.

INGREDIENTS • serves 4

1 3/4 oz butter
5 sheets brik pastry
8 fl oz (1 cup) pouring cream, chilled
½ sheet gelatin
9 oz cooked red beets
1 bunch radishes
Salt and pepper
3 1/2 oz lumpfish roe

PREPARATION TIME • 30 mins   ◆   COOKING TIME • 1 hr 30 mins

◆ Preheat the oven to 350°F. Place a bowl (to whip the cream) in the refrigerator or freezer to chill.

◆ Melt the butter. Make 20 cones out of aluminum foil. Lay out the sheets of brik pastry, brush them with the melted butter, then cut each one into four and roll the pieces into horns around the aluminum foil cones, buttered-side inside.

◆ Bake the cones, seam-side down, for 10 minutes, keeping an eye on them as they cook: the horns should be golden and crispy. Take them out of the oven, carefully remove the aluminum foil, and let them cool completely.

◆ Meanwhile, beat the cream in the chilled bowl until it forms soft peaks.

◆ Soften the gelatin in a bowl of warm water. Peel the beets and purée them in a food processor. Rinse the radishes, remove the tops and tails, and dice.

◆ Drain the gelatin and mix it into the puréed beets. Add the whipped cream and fold through until the mixture is a smooth mousse. Add the diced radishes.

◆ Taste and season lightly with salt and generously with pepper. Fill the cones with the mousse, finishing by adding 1 teaspoon of lumpfish roe in each.

Enjoy with friends . . . well . . . as long as you are quite certain they are not sinister creatures masquerading as friends, out to trap you.

Molecularized Smurf Spaghetti

In Soup a la Smurf, *Gargamel lists an impressive number of dishes in which Smurfs are the main ingredients. This is one of the dishes he kept in reserve. . . .*

PREPARATION TIME • 15 mins ◆ COOKING TIME • 45 mins

◆ Roll the lemons back and forth several times between your palm and a tabletop, pressing down firmly. Then flay the lemons with a grater or peeler to remove the zest. Cut them in half, and squeeze to collect the juice.

◆ Place the chicken in a dish, sprinkle over the zest and two-thirds of the lemon juice, cover, and marinate for the time it takes to cast a spell over the Smurfs.

◆ Catch the Smurfs. . . . Watch out! Too late . . . Wipe away the pepper thrown into your eyes by Jokey Smurf, bandage your fingers injured by Handy Smurf's hammer, and push Azrael out of the window, who has been watching the birds through the glass. Tie up the Smurfs so they don't escape and wash them, making sure to remove the glasses of Brainy Smurf first. Once they are tied together well, make them swallow a philosopher's potion to turn them into spaghetti.

◆ Peel the onion, cut it into small pieces, and cook with the rest of the lemon juice and a small glass of water over low heat for 20 minutes, until really soft. Meanwhile, heat 1 tablespoon of olive oil and 1 tablespoon of butter in a frying pan and add the drained pieces of chicken. Cook the cutlets (about 4 minutes per side), basting them regularly. Season with salt and pepper.

◆ Serve the Smurf spaghetti, warmed quickly in the microwave, with the chicken and stewed onions, and sprinkled with parsley leaves. (Author's note: no Smurfs were really harmed in the making of this recipe.)

INGREDIENTS • serves 4

2 lemons
4 chicken cutlets (you can also use leftover roast chicken)
5 1/2 oz live smurfs
(or 5 1/2 oz blue candy spaghetti)
1 onion
Olive oil and butter for frying
1 handful fresh parsley leaves
Salt and pepper

Dragon eggs

Be careful of what you wish for! If you think like a dragon, behave like a dragon, and by some chance end up sleeping in a dragon cave, you may well wake up one fine morning and find you have turned into one. Imagine what it would be like if you found yourself covered in scales, breathing fire, flying through the air, and guarding eggs like these!

INGREDIENTS • serves 4

1 lb 2 oz potatoes
1 onion
5 eggs
Salt and pepper
1 T chopped coriander leaves
Natural food colorings (beet juice, spinach juice, curry powder. . .)

Béchamel sauce
¾ oz butter
2 T flour
8 fl oz (1 cup) milk
Salt and pepper
¼ t turmeric

PREPARATION TIME • 15 mins ◆ COOKING TIME • 35 mins

RESTING TIME • 30 mins

◆ Preheat the oven to 350°F. Wash and peel the potatoes and grate them finely. Do the same with the onion (protect your eyes with a Dry-eye spell if necessary). Mix together the potatoes, onion, and 1 of the eggs. Season with salt and pepper. Divide this mixture between 8 tartlet pans, pressing it up the sides to make nests. Bake in the oven for 35 minutes.

◆ Meanwhile, cook the rest of the eggs for 9 minutes in boiling water, then plunge them in iced water to stop the cooking process. Tap each egg with the back of a spoon to break the shell without removing it.

◆ Place each egg in a freezer bag, then pour in a few drops of food coloring and 1 tablespoon of water so the egg is fully immersed in colored water. Let it rest for 20 minutes.

◆ Take the eggs out of the bags, peel them and place them in a bag containing a different coloring, if you wish. Let them rest for 10 minutes, then remove the eggs and drain them on paper towels.

◆ Make the béchamel sauce: Melt the butter and, when it starts to brown, add the flour. Cook for 2 minutes, then add the milk, stirring constantly to avoid lumps. Season with salt and pepper, add the turmeric, and cook for 5 minutes over low heat, stirring.

◆ Unmold the potato nests, fill them with sauce and a Dragon egg, and sprinkle with chopped cilantro.

RED DRAGON INN ROAST LAMB

One day when the cook was preparing a roast leg of lamb, the Dragon Inn was attacked by a troop of warriors from the ice lands. Legend has it that a small group fought valiantly to defend not just their lives but their meal, too! During the fight, a pot of sauce was tipped over the lamb that was cooking in the fireplace. Once peace had been restored, the warriors proclaimed it the best they had ever eaten!

INGREDIENTS • serves 6

2 cloves
½ t ground cinnamon
½ t ground cumin
½ t ground ginger
1 lamb leg roast (3 lb 5 oz)
2 garlic cloves
1 onion
1 carrot
Olive oil
4 T cider vinegar
6 T honey
Salt and pepper
1 bay leaf
2 T freshly picked rosemary leaves

PREPARATION TIME • 10 mins ◆ COOKING TIME • 7 hrs

RESTING TIME • 2 nights

◆ When night is falling over the narrow streets, when good people are returning to their homes and others emerging from their lairs, crush the cloves and mix them with the cinnamon, cumin, and ginger. Rub this mixture over the lamb, then wrap it in plastic wrap and let it stand overnight in the refrigerator.

◆ When the rays of dawn are caressing the roof of the inn, peel the garlic and onion (remove the sprout inside the garlic), then the carrot, and slice them all thinly.

◆ Heat some olive oil in a large cauldron or heavy-based pan and sear the lamb on all sides until browned all over. Remove from the pan and set aside.

◆ Sauté the garlic, onion and carrot in the pan for 5 minutes. Add 16 fl oz (2 cups) water and the cider vinegar, then the honey, and season with salt and pepper, stirring all the time so everything blends together well. Add the bay leaf and rosemary. Return the lamb to the pan and let it simmer for 7 hours over low heat, turning every hour and basting regularly with the sauce.

◆ Take the pan off the heat and let it cool completely. Return the cooled lamb to the refrigerator where no giant can detect its delicious aroma. The next day, gently reheat the lamb. Strain the cooking juices and serve with the meat before the dracs and trolls get too impatient and come to blows.

GARLIC TART

A delicious dish, ideal for a banquet between fighting arch enemies or for the chilly days of winter.

INGREDIENTS • serves 6

3 1/2 oz young garlic
1 clove
3 1/2 oz smoked bacon
10 1/2 oz plain *petit-suisse* cheese
1 3/4 oz raisins
2 eggs
Salt and pepper
9 oz shortcrust pastry
(from your bakery/cake shop)

PREPARATION TIME • 15 mins ◆ COOKING TIME • 1 hr 15 mins

◆ Preheat the oven to 350°F.

◆ When the wolves are howling and hunting deer around the castle, peel and remove the sprout from the middle of the garlic, then add it to a pot of boiling water with the clove. Cook for 30 minutes then remove the clove and carefully drain the garlic.

◆ Meanwhile, cut the bacon into slices and cook in a frying pan over high heat until the pieces are golden brown and crispy. Mix together the garlic, bacon, cheese, raisins, and eggs, and season lightly with salt (the bacon is already salty) and generously with pepper.

◆ Roll out the pastry, use it to line a tart pan, then fill with the garlic mixture. Bake for 45 minutes and enjoy before the next battle begins.

CARNUTES BOAR

Specially prepared by the Druids for their annual conference in the Forest of the Carnutes, this dish is also ideal in the fall, when indomitable Gauls from Brittany come to dinner. Serve with some magic potion!

INGREDIENTS • serves 4

1 3/4 oz honey

1 3/4 oz mustard seeds (or whole-grain mustard)

2 T mixture of chopped fresh thyme, rosemary, and parsley

Salt and pepper

10 1/2 oz boar fillets (or other part thick enough to carve slices from)

1 3/4 oz diced butter

3 onions

1 amphora of ale (1 bottle of dark beer)

3 T cranberries

PREPARATION TIME • 10 mins ◆ COOKING TIME • 1 hr 30 mins

◆ Preheat the oven to 350°F. Make a sauce by mixing together the honey, mustard, salt, pepper, and the herbs you picked fresh with dew at sunrise.

◆ Rub the meat with this mixture, place in a roasting pan, pour in a small glass of water, and add the diced butter. Place in the oven and cook for the time it takes for a quick chat between Druids (about 45 minutes), basting regularly with the juices.

◆ Peel the onions with a silver-bladed knife, then cut them into quarters. Try not to cry.

◆ Once the chat is finished, pour the ale over the boar and scrape around the meat well with a wooden spoon to collect and mix in any browned bits from the bottom of the pan. Add the pieces of onion and return to the oven for another 30 minutes, the time it takes a bard to chant a mystical rhyme.

◆ Arrange the cranberries around the boar, making sure they are well-covered in the sauce. Return the boar to the oven for another 15 minutes, or the time it takes to don your most becoming cambric tunic.

◆ Remove the boar from the oven, and let it rest for 10 minutes while the Druid elders make an interminable speech. Finally, enjoy the meal, chanting.

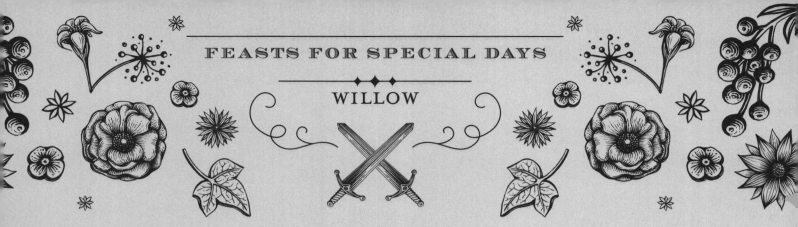

ROAST PORK WITH NELWYN VEGETABLES

This dish is specially prepared by the brave and loyal Willow Ufgood for the spring festival, where he hopes to be selected as a new apprentice by the High Aldwin.

INGREDIENTS • serves 6

6 carrots
2 parsnips
2 onions
2 garlic cloves
6 sage leaves
1 pork loin roast (2 1/4 lb)
Olive oil
1 T honey
Salt and pepper

PREPARATION TIME • 20 mins ◆ COOKING TIME • 1 hr 30 mins

◆ Wash and peel the carrots and parsnips, and slice them into rounds.

◆ Peel the onions and garlic, removing the sprout in the middle, and slice them very thinly.

◆ Rinse and shred the sage leaves.

◆ Brown the pork on all sides with a little oil in a flameproof casserole dish on high heat.

◆ Add the vegetables, the sage leaves, and a small glass of water, reduce the heat, and cook for 1 hour. Stir regularly, adding a little water if necessary and turning the roast every 20 minutes.

◆ After 50 minutes of cooking time, remove the lid from the casserole dish, stir in the honey, season with salt and pepper, and let it finish cooking uncovered.

Shadowy creature

Look closely—are you absolutely sure that this is a spicy turkey taco? Or has a much more fearsome creature taken its place while your back was turned? If leftover turkey can be transformed into a delicious dish to enjoy with friends, who knows what else it is capable of?

PREPARATION TIME • 10 mins   ◆   COOKING TIME • 1 hr 20 mins

◆ Rinse the chili peppers, cut them into four, and soak them for 1 hour in a large saucepan filled with boiling water.

◆ Strain the chili peppers and reserve the liquid but discard the skin and seeds. Peel and chop the onions and garlic cloves, first removing the sprout from the garlic.

◆ Blend the peeled and seeded chilis in a food processor with the garlic, onion, almonds, black sesame seeds, tomatoes, and spice mix, and season with salt and pepper.

◆ Pour the mixture into a saucepan over very low heat and thin out with the chicken broth, adding a little at a time and stirring. When it has a creamy consistency, add the cocoa powder and turkey pieces and cook for 5 minutes more.

◆ Warm the tortillas in the oven for 5 minutes. Fill the tortillas with the turkey, top with sauce, and serve hot.

Warning: Never read this recipe three times in a row under the light of a full moon; who knows what could happen . . .

INGREDIENTS • serves 4

10 dried mild chili peppers
2 onions
2 garlic cloves
2 3/4 oz almonds
2 T black sesame seeds
3 tomatoes
1 t quatre-épices spice mix (pepper, nutmeg, cinnamon, ginger)
Salt and pepper
16 fl oz (2 cups) chicken broth
1 3/4 oz unsweetened cocoa powder
10 1/2 oz leftover turkey (no bones)
4 corn tortillas

BEAUTY'S TARTLETS

The night that Belle arrives at the Beast's castle, her grief is so great that she refuses to eat. The invisible cooks use all of their creative culinary gifts to bring back her smile and appetite.

INGREDIENTS • makes 8 tartlets

9 oz shortcrust pastry (from your bakery/cake shop)
Flour for your work surface
3 1/2 oz porcini mushrooms
3 shallots
2 T fresh white breadcrumbs
1 egg
Juice of 1 lemon
Salt and Pepper
1 3/4 oz butter, melted

PREPARATION TIME • 15 mins ◆ COOKING TIME • 45 mins

◆ It can be a little disconcerting not to be able to see the servants when they have been rendered invisible under a spell. That is why it is recommended to prepare this recipe yourself.

◆ Preheat the oven to 350°F.

◆ Roll out the shortcrust pastry on a floured surface and cut out circles 1 1/4 inches wider than the diameter of your tartlet pans.

◆ Place the circles of pastry in the pans, crimping the edges for decoration. Place a piece of parchment paper inside the pastry shells, pour 1/2 inch of ceramic baking beans or dried beans on top of each, and bake blind for 25 minutes.

◆ Meanwhile, trim the base of the mushrooms, brush them carefully, clean with a damp cloth, and slice them thinly.

◆ Peel the shallots and chop them finely. Mix them with the breadcrumbs, egg, and lemon juice. Season with salt and pepper.

◆ Remove the tartlets from the oven, and remove the pieces of parchment paper and beans. Fill the tartlet cases with the shallot and breadcrumb mixture, lay the mushroom slices on top, and brush with melted butter. Bake for 20 minutes. Serve warm.

THE BEAST'S CHOPS

In his strange castle where torches and candelabra are fixed to the walls by human arms, the Beast initially refuses to join Beauty at mealtimes. But as time passes and their affection grows, they dine together and enjoy dishes that were popular in the seventeenth century—when Jeanne-Marie Leprince de Beaumont wrote the most popular version of this tale—such as these lamb chops with peas.

INGREDIENTS • serves 4

1 lb 2 oz fresh peas
3 1/2 oz spring onions
1 3/4 oz butter
8 lamb chops

Béchamel sauce
1 oz butter
1 oz flour
16 fl oz (2 cups) milk
Salt and pepper
2 T crème fraîche or sour cream
Turmeric

PREPARATION TIME • 10 mins ◆ COOKING TIME • 45 mins

◆ Preheat the oven to 450°F. Shell the peas and cook them for 4–5 minutes in a large saucepan of boiling water. Wash and peel the onions and cut them into thin strips.

◆ Heat a 4-ounce glass of water in a large pot, add the spring onions, and let them simmer for 10 minutes, then lower the heat and add 1 oz of the butter. Continue cooking for another 15 minutes, then drain.

◆ Melt the remaining butter, brush it over the chops, place them in a baking dish, and cook them in the oven for 20 minutes. At the end of this time, wrap them in a sheet of aluminum foil and let them rest for 5 minutes.

◆ Meanwhile, make the béchamel sauce: Melt the butter and, when it starts to brown, add the flour. Cook for 2 minutes, then add the milk, stirring constantly to avoid lumps. Season with salt and pepper, add the turmeric, and cook for 5 minutes on low heat, stirring.

◆ Add the spring onions, season with salt and pepper, and cook for 5 minutes over low heat, still stirring. Stir in the crème fraîche or sour cream. Serve the chops with the peas and sauce.

◆ The fact that the dishes sometimes appear and disappear from the table by themselves is just something you get used to.

CHAPTER III

MARVELOUS SNACKS AND SWEETS

The Eye of Agamotto

The long initiation period of Dr. Strange's young disciple is at an end. He is finally prepared to counter the forces of evil and Baron Mordo. To assist him in this task, the doctor gives him two mystical items that will be very useful: the Cloak of Levitation and the Eye of Agamotto, the amulet with clairvoyant powers. May it never fall into the wrong hands!

INGREDIENTS • 8 cookies

The cookie dough
5 1/2 oz flour + extra for work surface
2 3/4 oz superfine sugar
3 pinches ground cinnamon
2 3/4 oz butter
1 egg

The cream
4 fl oz (1/2 cup) pouring cream (30% dairy fat)
4 1/2 oz mascarpone cheese
1 t vanilla powder
1 3/4 oz white chocolate

Decoration
3 1/2 oz raspberries

PREPARATION TIME • 1 hr ◆ COOKING TIME • 15 mins

RESTING TIME • 30 mins

◆ Preheat the oven to 350°F.

◆ Place the flour, sugar, and cinnamon in a mixing bowl. Swirl it all together using the Cloak of Levitation.

◆ Cut the butter into pieces and add it to the flour. Rub between your fingers tips until the mixture looks like coarse meal.

◆ Beat the egg in a bowl, then add it to the dough. Lay the Cloak of Levitation over the dough and let it rest in the refrigerator for 30 minutes.

◆ On a floured surface, roll out the dough to 5mm and cut out 8 circles with a cookie cutter.

◆ Using the offcuts, roll small balls of dough and place them around the edge of the circles.

◆ Bake in the oven for 10 minutes and allow to cool.

◆ Place the cream, mascarpone, and vanilla in a bowl. Beat everything together until firm peaks form by creating a tornado or using a whisk.

◆ Use your mystical powers to melt the white chocolate in a water bath (or see page 121) and fold it gently into the cream.

◆ Complete the amulets of Agamotto by piping the cream in the shape of an eye and adding a raspberry for the iris.

POISONED APPLES

Delicious and irresistible. . . . These apples are ideal if, like the witch from Snow White, you think that the best way to ensure that an act of revenge is carried out properly is to do it yourself.

INGREDIENTS • serves 4

4 Granny Smith apples
1 lemon
1 lb 2 oz fructose (health food section of your store)
Blue and black liquid food coloring

PREPARATION TIME • 5 mins   ◆   COOKING TIME • 10 mins

RESTING TIME • 15 mins

◆ Conjure up some lightning in your secret laboratory so you can see more clearly, then summon the spirit of the Mirror.

◆ Rinse the apples, remove the stems and insert wooden twigs or sticks into the center, pushing them in well so they are secure.

◆ Roll the lemon back and forth several times across a work surface under the palm of your hand, pressing firmly, then cut it in half and collect the juice.

◆ In a cauldron as black as your soul, melt the fructose with the lemon juice and bring to a boil. When the candy is golden but not yet coppery, add 4 drops of blue coloring to each 1 drop of black (according to the Mirror's advice).

◆ Mix and remove from the heat.

◆ Dip the apples in the candy, coating them completely with both the sugar and your resentment.

◆ Place the apples on a plate lined with parchment paper and let them cool completely, until the candy is as dry as your heart.

Toast
FOR DISOBEDIENT CHILDREN

When Mr. Brown's children finally admitted that life was much better when they listened to Nanny McPhee, she made them this toast, which they all agreed was delicious.

PREPARATION TIME • 15 mins ◆ COOKING TIME • 20 mins

INGREDIENTS • serves 6

2 pears
4 1/2 oz hazelnuts
1 3/4 oz butter
1 1/2 oz honey
1 oz raisins
½ t ground cinnamon
6 eggs
6 slices artisan-style bread

◆ Ask Mrs. Blatherwick to peel the pears and cut them into small cubes with sides measuring exactly 0.43 inches. Roughly crush the hazelnuts.

◆ Go in search of the last frying pan the Brown children have not turned into a gong or a tennis racquet, and melt half of the butter. Pour in the honey and let it caramelize for a few moments, then add the pieces of pear, hazelnuts, raisins, and cinnamon. Mix gently so the honey coats all the ingredients.

◆ Let the mixture cook for 10 minutes, the time it takes you to check that the children are at last playing nicely in the parlor (without jumping on the seats or painting the baby blue).

◆ Break the eggs into a bowl and lightly beat them together. Add the rest of the butter to the frying pan and add the beaten eggs. Let them cook for 2 or 3 minutes before gently shaking the pan so the omelet doesn't stick.

◆ Cook for 5 to 8 minutes in total, while Evangeline toasts the slices of bread, then slide the omelet onto a large plate, folding it like a turnover.

◆ Cut the omelet into six pieces, slide one onto each piece of toasted bread, add a spoonful of fruit, nut, and honey mixture, and enjoy, ignoring the whispers and giggles of the children who claim that even this morning your face was still festooned with warts and a mustache. . . . Ri-di-cul-ous!

MARY POPPINS

Raspberry cakes

Mary Poppins has a real passion for raspberry cakes. She adores eating them with her friend Bert when they take afternoon tea inside one of his pictures.

PREPARATION TIME • 15 mins ◆ COOKING TIME • 8 mins

INGREDIENTS • 16 cakes

2 3/4 oz butter
2 eggs
2 3/4 oz flour
1 t baking powder
2 3/4 oz superfine sugar
3 1/2 oz raspberry purée
(in the baby food section of your store)

◆ Preheat the oven to 450°F.

◆ While Bert makes one of his chalk drawings, melt the butter and let it cool to warm. Break the eggs into a mixing bowl and beat them together quickly. For increased efficiency, ask the whisk to do the beating by itself.

◆ While Bert draws a green meadow with a stream trickling across it, beneath the eyes of the delighted children, take the opportunity to sift the flour and baking powder into the bowl with the beaten egg, and mix together. Add the sugar and mix again, then pour in the melted butter and mix once more.

◆ While the children point out that they can see horses racing across the meadow, pour a spoonful of the batter into each hole of a madeleine mold. Next, add a teaspoon of raspberry purée and cover with more cake batter, filling the holes by two-thirds only to avoid overflowing during baking.

◆ Bake for 4 minutes, lower the temperature to 350°F, and bake for a further 4 minutes.

◆ Turn out the madeleines and let them cool just for the time it takes to pick up an umbrella, put on your coat, and jump into the picture, too.

MARY POPPINS

STRAWBERRY ICE CREAM

Everyone knows that Mary Poppins is a model nanny. Under her care, children would never dance a wild jig across the rooftops of London, buy sweets in an invisible shop, ride a carousel in a picture drawn on the ground, or slide backward down the bannister. You can rest assured that none of this would happen. But I am going to share with you one of Mary's secrets: this wonderful strawberry ice cream. There's nothing like it to reward well-behaved children and ensure they stay that way . . . at least for a little while.

PREPARATION TIME • 15 mins ◆ FREEZING TIME • 1 night

INGREDIENTS • makes 6 ice creams

1 lb 2 oz strawberries
1 lb 2 oz superfine sugar
8 fl oz (1 cup) spring water
Juice of 1 lemon
1 lb 2 oz whipped cream

◆ Rinse and remove the stems of the strawberries. Set 6 strawberries aside and finely dice them.

◆ Mash the rest of the strawberries to a purée.

◆ Pour the sugar into a dish and dissolve it in the spring water and lemon juice, mixing well.

◆ Incorporate the whipped cream, strawberry purée, and diced strawberries and mix again.

◆ Pour into ice pop molds or six small yogurt tubs, and let stand in the refrigerator overnight or until Admiral Boom fires his cannon.

SCOURER REPELLENTS

The infamous Scourers made witch-hunting their specialty. But fortunately for the magical community, a certain Dunbarion Bluemountain created these repellents, rendering witches and wizards totally undetectable to any Scourers hunting in the vicinity.

INGREDIENTS
• makes about 20 foils

2 1/4 lb tomatoes, very ripe
2 T balsamic vinegar
8 sheets gelatin
7 oz popping sugar

PREPARATION TIME • 15 mins ◆ REFRIGERATION TIME • 2 hrs

◆ Rinse the tomatoes in a large quantity of water, without flooding your laboratory.

◆ Submerge the tomatoes for 2 minutes in a saucepan of boiling water (or cast a Geyserpuff spell), then purée in a food processor.

◆ Carefully strain the liquid; it mustn't contain any leaves or bits of stem.

◆ Pour the liquid into a cauldron, add the balsamic vinegar, and heat gently, adding the sheets of gelatin one by one. Once the gelatin is completely dissolved, pour into a dish lined with parchment paper and let it rest for 2 hours in the refrigerator.

◆ Pour the popping sugar into a bowl.

◆ Turn out the tray of tomato gelatin onto a work surface covered with parchment paper. Cut out 1 1/2-inch squares and roll them in the popping sugar.

◆ Keep the repellents away from moisture and pop one in your mouth as soon as you get wind of approaching Scourers.

TREACLE TART

Never mind that you have to face an uncooperative dragon at a Triwizard Tournament or that your best friends are quarreling, do as Harry does: enjoy a slice of treacle tart and forget your troubles till not a crumb is left.

INGREDIENTS • serves 8

The pastry

7 oz flour + extra for work surface
3 1/2 oz butter, cut into pieces
1 egg
1 pinch salt

The filling

15 fl oz golden syrup
(international food section of your store)
2 1/4 oz butter, cut into pieces
Juice of 1 lemon
5 1/2 oz breadcrumbs (or cornflakes)

PREPARATION TIME • 20 mins ◆ COOKING TIME • 1 hr

RESTING TIME • 30 mins

◆ Sift the flour into a bowl containing 1 1/2 oz of the butter, cut into pieces, and rub together with your fingertips. When the mixture looks like coarse meal, add the egg and the salt, and 3 or 4 tablespoons of water collected from the lake on a starry night. Mix together well, roll into a ball, cover with plastic wrap, and let rest in the refrigerator for 30 minutes.

◆ Preheat the oven to 350°F.

◆ Roll out the dough on a floured surface to a thickness of 1/8 inch and lay it in a round buttered tart ring. Prick the base using a fork, or simply use a Hedgehog-Roller spell. Lay a sheet of parchment paper on top, cover with ceramic baking beans or dried beans, and bake blind for 20 minutes.

◆ Remove the beans and sheet of parchment paper.

◆ Lower the oven temperature to 325°F.

◆ In a small cauldron or pan on low heat, melt the golden syrup, then add the remaining butter, cut into pieces, and the lemon juice. Take the pan off the heat, mix in the breadcrumbs or cornflakes, and pour into the tart base.

◆ Bake for 20 minutes in the oven, then lower the temperature to 275°F and bake for another 15 to 20 minutes, until the tart is golden brown and the filling soft.

◆ Let it cool and serve with whipped cream.

WEREWOLF BISCUITS

A werewolf never turns its snout up at a good, crunchy meal. The ideal of course would be a "real" werewolf meal, a fresh and juicy human for example. As a substitute, these sweet "dog biscuits" with a drizzle of syrup will still have him licking his chops.

INGREDIENTS • serves 4

7 oz shortbread cookies
1 oz butter, melted
7 oz sweetened whipped cream
7 oz semisweet chocolate
Sugar, as needed
1 jar (or approximately 17 ounces) black cherries in syrup (morello cherries . . .)

PREPARATION TIME • 10 mins ◆ COOKING TIME • 15 mins

RESTING TIME • 15 mins

◆ Begin by crushing the shortbread cookies to very fine crumbs in a bowl. Melt the butter and mix with the crumbs, then place 4 pastry rings, 3 1/4 inches in diameter, on plates and pack the crumbs inside, pressing them down to make bases. Place the plates in the refrigerator for 15 minutes.

◆ Place the whipped cream in a bowl. Gently melt the chocolate in another bowl (see page 121) and let it cool to just warm. Mix it into the whipped cream, not forgetting to taste and add some sugar if necessary. Place in the refrigerator with the bases.

◆ Now drain the cherries, pouring the juice into a small pan, and set aside the cherries. Boil the juice hard for 15 minutes until it becomes thick and syrupy.

◆ Take the bases out of the refrigerator, remove the rings, and place some cherries in a circle on top (set a few aside for decoration).

◆ Take a piping bag (or a freezer bag with a corner cut off), fill with the chocolate cream, and pipe over the cherries. Decorate with the remaining cherries, pressing them on lightly so they don't fall off. Finish by adding a generous spoonful of the cherry syrup on top of each dessert. Serve immediately.

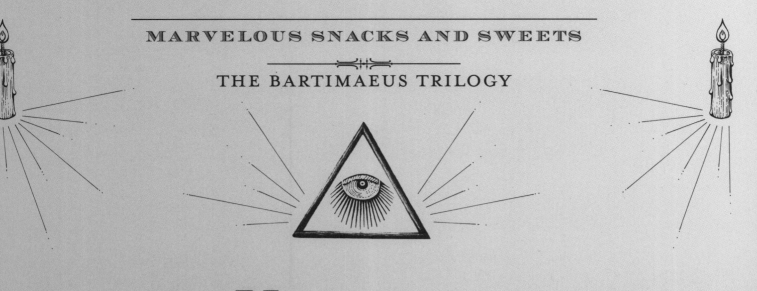

NATHANIEL'S REMINDERS

Before he was known as John Mandrake, Nathaniel, the youngest minister of all time, was a small boy who, like all children of his age, loved sweet things. The only difference was that he also possessed extraordinary magical gifts. So what could be better than these delicious magic wands to take him back, as if by magic, to the sweetness of childhood?

INGREDIENTS • 10 lollipops

9 oz pumpkin, peeled
(frozen if out of season)
9 oz flour + extra for work surface
1 pinch salt
1 T ground hazelnuts
3 1/2 oz butter
2 T maple syrup
1 egg yolk, for glazing

PREPARATION TIME • 20 mins   ◆   COOKING TIME • 45 mins

RESTING TIME • 15 mins

◆ Steam the pumpkin for 25 minutes, until it is easily pierced with the tip of a knife, then place it in a strainer and let it drain.

◆ Sift the flour and salt into a bowl, add the ground hazelnuts, 4 fl oz (1/2 cup) lukewarm water and the diced butter, and mix together. Knead until you have a smooth, non-sticky dough, adding a little more water or flour if too dry or sticky. Wrap the dough in plastic wrap and let it rest for 15 minutes in the refrigerator.

◆ Meanwhile, preheat the oven to 350°F and mash the pumpkin to a smooth purée. Add the maple syrup.

◆ Flour a work surface, roll the dough out thinly (about 1/8 inch) and cut out whatever shapes you like using a cookie cutter. Place one teaspoon of pumpkin purée in the middle of each shape, then place a lollipop stick on top, cover with a second pastry shape, and seal the edges by pressing them gently together with a fork.

◆ Place the lollipops on a baking sheet, brush with a little egg yolk, and bake for 25 minutes: they should be golden brown, not copper-colored.

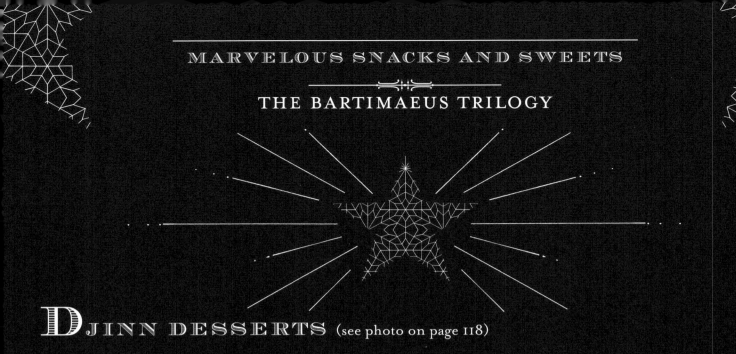

DJINN DESSERTS (see photo on page 118)

How is it that Bartimaeus has come to find himself making pastries for an ill-tempered wizard? He was sent to this boot camp for disobedient djinn by the great King Solomon—bounteous be his beard!

PREPARATION TIME • 15 mins ◆ COOKING TIME • 15 mins

◆ Preheat the oven to 300°F.

◆ While trying to forget that Khaba the Cruel Magician has a silly air about him, melt 1 oz butter in a hot frying pan and add the dates and sesame seeds. Heat for 5 minutes on low heat and set aside.

◆ Sift the flour and baking powder, add the salt, then 9 oz softened butter, and knead everything together. Add the egg, then 1 cup milk, and mix again until you have a smooth, malleable dough.

◆ Divide the dough into about 20 equal pieces. Form each piece into a small ball, hold it in the palm of your hand, and make a hole in the center using a spoon. Fill with some of the date mixture and close it up. Repeat until all the dough balls are filled.

◆ Place the balls on a sheet of parchment paper, brush with milk, and bake for 15 minutes. Take the opportunity to quietly slip outside to enjoy some fresh air with the other djinn. Devour.

INGREDIENTS

• **Makes about 20 balls**

9 oz butter, softened + 1 oz for the dates

7 oz dates, mashed

2 T toasted sesame seeds

2 1/4 lb flour

1 t baking powder

1 pinch salt

1 egg

8 fl oz (1 cup) milk + a little for brushing on pastry

CHOCOLATE FROGS

On board the Hogwarts Express, *Ron introduces Harry to magic confectioneries. It was when he opened a box of chocolate frogs that Harry discovered a card bearing the name Albus Dumbledore, the famous headmaster of Hogwarts. These frogs are an unmissable treat in the world of magic; you just have to make sure they don't jump too far.*

PREPARATION TIME • 20 mins ◆ RESTING TIME • 3 hrs

INGREDIENTS • serves 6

1 3/4 oz milk chocolate
1 3/4 oz semisweet chocolate
2 3/4 oz marshmallows
Frog-shaped molds

◆ Break the chocolate into large pieces using a Crackling spell and place them in a heatproof bowl. Make a water bath to melt the chocolate. Fill a large pan partway with water, then place the heatproof bowl on top—it should be smaller than the pan but wide enough that its base is suspended in the water, but not touching the bottom of the pan.

◆ Place the pan over a gentle heat until the chocolate melts. (Make sure that there is enough water in the pan to heat the bowl.) Divide the melted chocolate carefully between the frog-shaped molds so that it coats the insides thoroughly. Turn the molds over on a sheet of parchment paper to allow the excess chocolate to run off. Let the frog cases chill in the refrigerator for 30 minutes.

◆ Gently melt the marshmallows with a little water in a saucepan over a gentle heat until smooth and creamy.

◆ Take the frog cases out of the refrigerator, fill them with melted marshmallow, smoothing the top with a spoon, and set aside again in the refrigerator for at least 2 hours (the longer the frogs stay in the refrigerator, the better they are).

◆ Collect and melt the leftover chocolate as before, carefully cover the marshmallow filling with it, smoothing with a knife, and set aside for 30 more minutes in the refrigerator.

◆ Unmold carefully and utter the Wrigglish spell to bring the frogs to life.

ELVEN WAYBREAD (LEMBAS)

Wrapped in long leaves, these fortifying and nourishing cookies allow the Elves and their friends to survive in arid lands. It was Lembas that gave Frodo and Sam sustenance in their crossing of Mordor, to throw the Ring into Mount Doom and thus defeat Sauron.

INGREDIENTS
• Makes about 20 cookies

1 lb 2 oz flour + extra for work surface
9 oz light soft brown sugar
8 fl oz (1 cup) water collected from the leaves of a golden tree
1 pinch salt
4 1/2 oz nuts, shelled (almonds, walnuts, hazelnuts . . .)
4 1/2 oz dried fruit
(raisins, figs, apples. . . .)

PREPARATION TIME • 20 mins ◆ COOKING TIME • 20 mins

◆ Preheat the oven to 350°F.

◆ Sift the flour into a pottery bowl fired during two equinoxes, then add the sugar, water, and salt. Mix well to make a smooth, homogenous dough.

◆ Break the nuts into small pieces. Dice the dried fruit into squares of about 1/2 inch.

◆ Using a rolling pin, roll out the dough on a floured work surface to a thickness of 1/2 inch, remembering to prick it with a fork so no bubbles form while it cooks.

◆ Cut the dough into squares half a Hobbit palm wide (about 2 inches).

◆ Place the cookies on a sheet of parchment paper, then sprinkle with the dried fruit and nuts. Bake for 10 minutes. Brush the top of the cookies with a little water or dew collected from the leaves of a golden tree, to form a lovely crust, and cook for another 10 minutes.

◆ Let the waybread cool before wrapping it up for your journey.

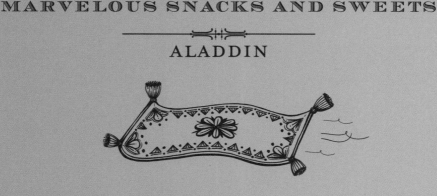

JAFAR'S JEWELS

Sound the trumpets and bang the drums! Make way for the great Jafar! May all bow down before him, or they will end up in chains! Speaking of which, the great Jafar is especially fond of these delicious little cookies.

PREPARATION TIME • 15 mins ◆ COOKING TIME • 20 mins

INGREDIENTS
• **makes about 20 rings**

11 1/2 oz flour, sifted
1/4 oz baking powder
9 oz honey
2 egg whites
2 1/4 oz butter, melted
1 oz ground hazelnuts

◆ Send your most faithful servant to light the oven at 400°F.

◆ In a bowl scrubbed clean of all traces of poison (you can never be too careful!), mix the sifted flour and baking powder with the honey.

◆ Seize a whisk and beat the egg whites savagely in another bowl (make sure it is clean, dry, and grease-free). When firm peaks form, add the butter, melted under the midday sun, and mix in gently.

◆ Pour the beaten egg whites onto the flour-honey mixture and knead together until the dough is smooth and puts up no more resistance (if it sticks a little, throw in a little flour; if it is too thick, have it drink a little water).

◆ Take a walnut-sized piece of dough, flatten it with your hand, and make a hole in the middle with the handle of a wooden spoon. Turn the handle to enlarge the hole. Repeat until you run out of dough.

◆ Place the cookies on a sheet of parchment paper and scatter with the hazelnuts. Bake for 15 to 20 minutes until golden brown.

◆ Once they are cold, thread them onto a cord to wear over your shoulder, so they are easy to reach when you are feeling peckish, without having to get down from your horse or your flying carpet.

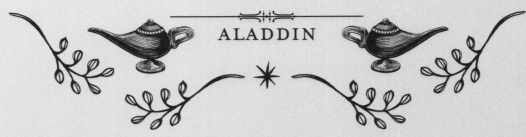

DELIGHTS OF THE LAMP

It is true that spending 1,001 nights in a lamp gives you time to fine-tune your recipes. When you taste thes small delicacies from the Orient you will soon be singing their praises!

PREPARATION TIME • 20 mins   ◆   COOKING TIME • 15 mins

RESTING TIME • 15 mins

◆ Caravan drivers with their camels cross miles of dusty desert to eat these pastries! To you, my Friend, I will reveal their secret.

◆ Make the pastry by rubbing together the sifted flour and butter with your fingertips, until the mixture resembles the sand of the dunes, then stir in the superfine sugar. Next, add the cinnamon and confectioners' sugar and let it rest for the time it takes you to go and smell the roses of the Sultan.

◆ Place the almonds in a pan over a gentle heat without letting your mind wander, or else they will burn! And when they have turned the color of the sand of the oasis at sunrise . . . What's that? You have never gazed upon the oasis at sunrise? Remind me to take you there. So, when the almonds are golden brown, grind them finely and mix them with the sugar, cinnamon, orange flower water, and rose petals. Shape the mixture into small balls.

◆ Heat the oven to 350°F.

◆ Using a rolling pin or rolled-up carpet, roll out the pastry dough 4mm thick on a floured surface and using an upturned glass or a cookie cutter, cut out an even number of circles from the dough. Place a ball of filling on half of the circles and place a second circle of pastry on top, sealing the edges so that the mischievous filling does not escape. Bake your little pastries in the oven for about 15 minutes.

◆ Be careful, my Friend, make sure they stay a light brown. Otherwise they will become hard like the pebbles on the edge of the oasis at sunrise. You still don't know? Well then, we will go there tomorrow on my best flying carpet!

INGREDIENTS
• **Makes about 20 delights**

The pastry
1 lb 2 oz flour + extra for work surface
7 oz butter, softened
3 T superfine sugar
1 t ground cinnamon
2 T confectioners' sugar

The filling
1 lb 2 oz sliced almonds
7 oz superfine sugar
1 t ground cinnamon
1 T orange flower water
1 3/4 oz crystallized rose petals

Magica de Spell's Lucky Dimes

When she fails to steal Scrooge's Number One Dime, Magica De Spell consoles herself by nibbling these cookies.

PREPARATION TIME • 10 mins   ◆   COOKING TIME • 20 mins

RESTING TIME • 15 mins

INGREDIENTS • serves 4

9 oz chestnut flour
4 1/2 oz confectioners' sugar
4 1/2 oz butter, softened
1 pinch salt
2 1/4 oz ground almonds
1 vanilla bean
1 egg yolk, for glazing

◆ Spread out a very thin layer of the flour in a nonstick frying pan and toast it for a few minutes on high heat (2 to 5 minutes, depending on the thickness of the layer).

◆ Let the flour cool, then sift it into a bowl and mix with the confectioners' sugar, softened butter, salt, and ground almonds.

◆ Cut the vanilla bean in half lengthwise, scrape out the seeds with the back of a knife, and add them to the mixture.

◆ Roll out the dough between two sheets of parchment paper until it is as thin as an authentic florin (about 1/8 inch), then place the dough and paper in the refrigerator for 15 minutes to firm up.

◆ Preheat the oven to 325°F. Cut out circles in the dough with a glass or circular cookie cutter and place them on a baking sheet. Brush with beaten egg yolk and bake for 12 to 15 minutes until they are golden brown.

MELUSINE

FAIRY MELUSINE'S PASTRY

The fairy Melusine, condemned to become part-woman, part-serpent every Saturday and stay out of sight of her husband, gets a little bored on her French estate. What better way of passing the time than to make this delicious pastry to add some magic to her day?

PREPARATION TIME • 15 mins ◆ COOKING TIME • 45 mins

REFRIGERATION TIME • 30 mins

INGREDIENTS • serves 6

7 oz pitted prunes

1 egg + 1 egg yolk for glazing

3 1/2 oz superfine sugar + 1 T for prunes

4 1/2 oz butter, softened

9 oz flour + extra for work surface

1 t baking powder

1 pinch salt

◆ Soak the prunes in a bowl of lukewarm water for 30 minutes. Beat 1 egg with the 3 1/2 oz sugar in a bowl until the mixture becomes pale, then add the butter and mix together vigorously. Sift the flour, baking powder, and salt, then add to the first mixture and mix again. Shape the dough into a ball, wrap it in plastic wrap, and place it in the refrigerator for 30 minutes.

◆ Meanwhile, drain the prunes and place them with 1 tablespoon sugar in a saucepan over low heat. Let them cook for 15 minutes, mashing them roughly with a fork.

◆ Preheat the oven to 375°F. Take the ball of dough out of the refrigerator and divide it into two equal portions. Roll out each portion on a floured work surface using a rolling pin to make two circles about 8 inches in diameter.

◆ Place a sheet of parchment paper on a baking sheet and place the first circle of pastry on top. Spread the cooked prunes over the circle to about 5/8 inch inside the edge.

◆ Brush around the edge with a little water, then cover with the second circle of pastry. Press the edges down lightly to seal them as well as you can so the prune mixture can't escape (use the tines of a fork if you need to). Brush the top with beaten egg yolk and bake for 30 minutes. Allow it to cool completely, then enjoy under the midnight sun.

Patapumpkins

Patapumpkins are a favorite candy of witches and wizards. Enjoyed at home by the whole family since the beginning of time and in schools of magic by generations of pupils, the rumor goes that certain teachers love them to the point of making Patapumpkins one of their favorite passwords! Traditionally made with love for Halloween, try making this dish from different varieties of pumpkin: a real delicacy!

PREPARATION TIME • 5 mins   ◆   COOKING TIME • 10 mins

RESTING TIME • 2 hrs

INGREDIENTS • Makes 1 lb 2 oz

9 oz pumpkin (try different varieties . . .)
11 1/2 oz jam-making sugar
1 squeeze lemon juice
Superfine sugar, to finish

◆ Don your protective gloves, and using a Rapidrinder spell, remove the rind of the pumpkin. Cut the flesh into chunks, then chop into small pieces in a food processor.

◆ Place a small plate in the freezer or cast a level-3 Chill spell.

◆ Place the pumpkin, jam-making sugar, and lemon juice in a medium-sized cauldron and bring to a boil. Stir constantly, chanting, until the sugar has completely dissolved (this is essential for the recipe to succeed).

◆ After letting the pumpkin mixture simmer for 10 minutes, take the plate out of the freezer, drop a little mixture onto it, count to ten, and turn the plate up so it is vertical. The mixture is ready if it stays firmly in place as a paste. If it runs, keep simmering and repeat the test.

◆ Place a sheet of parchment paper on a tray, overhanging the edges, then pour in the pumpkin mixture and let it cool for at least 2 hours.

◆ Once the paste has completely cooled, cut out your patapumpkins using a pumpkin-shaped cookie cutter (or a homemade cardboard stencil), then roll them in superfine sugar so the candy won't stick to your fingers.

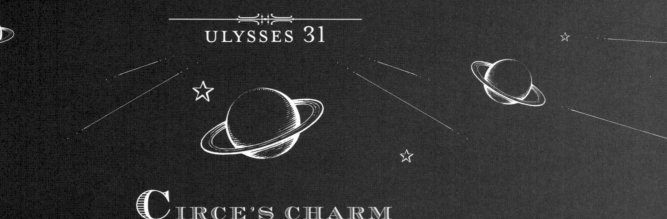

ULYSSES 31

CIRCE'S CHARM

In the TV series Ulysses 31, *Circe the enchantress wants to gather under one roof all the knowledge of the universe. She lures the crews of passing ships to her planet and puts them under a spell during an elaborate meal so that they stay with her forever and help her build up her intergalatic library.*

PREPARATION TIME • 15 mins ◆ RESTING TIME • 1 hr

COOKING TIME • 20 mins ◆ REFRIGERATION TIME • 30 mins

INGREDIENTS • serves 4

2 3/4 oz flour
1 t baking powder
2 eggs
1 pinch salt
2 3/4 oz superfine sugar
9 oz plain fromage blanc
3 3/4 oz crème fraîche (30% dairy fat)
3 1/2 oz honey
1 sheet of gelatin

Star date 2063.05.04 — Ship's log of the Odysseus.
We were drawn in at subluminal speed by an unidentified singularity which turned out to be the library-planet of Circe. My shipmates Telemachus and Yumi, protected by our droid Nono, went out to expore and were captured, tempted by a dessert. I am entering the recipe (translated into the common language) into the databank of Shirka, our shipboard computer.

◆ Preheat the oven to 350°F.

◆ Sift the flour and baking powder. Break the eggs, separating the whites from the yolks. In a clean, dry bowl, beat the whites to firm peaks with the salt, add the sugar, and beat again. Pour in both egg yolks at once. Fold them in very gently, incorporating as much air as possible. Fold in the flour and baking powder.

◆ Pour into an 8-inch square pan and bake in the oven for 20 minutes. Let it cool completely before unmolding.

◆ Whisk the fromage blanc and crème fraîche together until smooth and creamy. Set aside in the refrigerator. Melt the honey and gelatin in a saucepan over very low heat.

◆ Place the génoise cake on a plate, trim it to the dimensions of the cake mold, and place at the bottom. Pour the chilled cream over top of it.

◆ Place in a cooling cell for 30 minutes.

Witches' Council Jello Ring

This is a fresh and fruity version of the typical 1960s dessert, perfect for impressing all your housewitch friends at the next Tupperware party.

PREPARATION TIME • 15 mins ◆ COOKING TIME • 15 mins

REFRIGERATION TIME • 3 hrs

INGREDIENTS • serves 6

16 fl oz (2 cups) pomegranate juice
8 sheets of gelatin
16 fl oz (2 cups) soda
1 lb 2 oz berries, according to the season of the Witches' Council

◆ When the moon is waxing, heat the pomegranate juice in a saucepan.

◆ When the first bubbles appear, lower the heat and add the gelatin sheets, stirring until they are completely dissolved. Let the liquid cool for a quarter of an hour in mortal time, then add the soda and stir again.

◆ Rinse the berries and remove any stems if necessary.

◆ Pour the liquid into a 10 1/2-inch ring mold, distribute the berries around the mold, and let it set in the refrigerator for 3 hours, or ideally a whole day. Serve chilled.

ALAKAZAM COOKIES

In the film The Sword in the Stone, *Merlin is a wizard living with his pet owl Archimedes in a cottage in the middle of the forest. Predicting exactly when Wart—his nickname for the future King Arthur—will arrive, Merlin organizes an afternoon tea for his young protégé.*

PREPARATION TIME • 5 mins   ◆   COOKING TIME • 15 mins

RESTING TIME • 30 mins

INGREDIENTS • serves 4

1 3/4 oz sesame seeds
7 oz buckwheat flour
2 3/4 oz superfine sugar
1 pinch salt
1 t ground cinnamon
2 eggs
2 1/2 oz butter, softened

◆ Oyez, oyez!

◆ I give you the recipe for alakazam cookies, favored by our noble liege lord King Arthur! Invented by the great Merlin himself for the pleasure of young and old!

◆ Toast the sesame seeds in a pan for a few minutes over high heat. Remove and set aside.

◆ Mix the flour with the sugar, salt, cinnamon, and sesame seeds, then the eggs and softened butter. Roll out the dough between two sheets of parchment paper to a thickness of about 1/8 inch.

◆ Rest it in the refrigerator for at least 30 minutes so it firms up.

◆ Preheat the oven to 350°F.

◆ Cut out rectangular cookies (2 x 2 3/4 inches), sprinkle the reserved sesame seeds on top, and cook in the oven for 10 to 15 minutes.

TITANIA'S DELIGHT

Titania, the Queen of the Fairies, likes to amuse herself with Oberon, the King, holding banquets where the spirits of the forest indulge in delicious fruit-based desserts.

PREPARATION TIME • 5 mins

- Begin by washing and removing the stems of the fruits.

- Submerge the peaches for 1 minute in boiling water, then remove their skin and stones. Next, pit the cherries, and plums.

- Cut the cherries in two and dice the peaches and plums.

- Break the meringues into small pieces.

- Assemble the layers of the dessert in the following way: a first layer of blue fruits (blackcurrants, blueberries, or blackberries), followed by 1 layer of meringue, and 1 layer of whipped cream.

- Continue in the same way, alternating layers of fruit, meringue, and whipped cream, making sure to place the fruit in the following order of color: blue, red, orange, yellow, and, finally, green.

- Finish by sprinkling roughly crushed toasted hazelnuts on the top layer of whipped cream.

INGREDIENTS • serves 4

3 1/2 oz yellow peaches (or apricots, melons)

3 1/2 oz cherries (or strawberries, raspberries)

3 1/2 oz greengage plums (or kiwifruit)

4 meringues (from your local bakery)

3 1/2 oz black currants (or ripe blueberries, blackberries)

8 fl oz (1 cup) whipped cream (or yogurt for a lighter version)

3 1/2 oz gooseberries (or white peaches)

2 1/4 oz toasted and roughly crushed hazelnuts

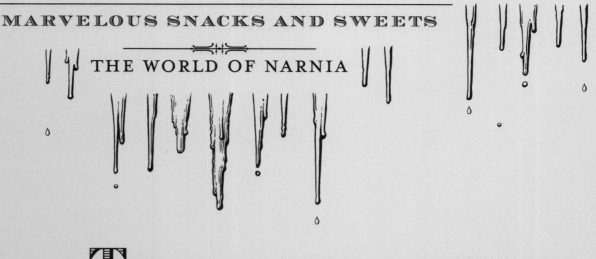

THE WHITE WITCH'S TURKISH DELIGHT

When Edmund Pevensie enters Narnia for the first time through the magic wardrobe, he meets the White Witch. To win the young boy over, she offers him the best Turkish delight that he has ever tasted.

PREPARATION TIME • 15 mins ◆ COOKING TIME • 55 mins

RESTING TIME • 1 night

INGREDIENTS • makes 20 pieces

2 3/4 oz cornstarch + more for sifting
10 1/2 oz superfine sugar
1 t lemon juice
1 T rosewater
1 glass confectioners' sugar
Neutral-flavored oil

◆ While Lucy, Peter, and Susan remain hidden between the coats inside the magic wardrobe, blend 2 3/4 oz cornstarch with 5 fl oz (2/3 cup) water in a bowl and set aside.

◆ Bring the superfine sugar, lemon juice, and 4 fl oz (1/2 cup) water to a boil in a saucepan. When the syrup reaches 240°F, add all the cornstarch mixture at once, stirring constantly with a wooden spoon. Simmer for about 50 minutes over low heat, continuing to stir. The paste is ready when the light from the street lamp no longer illuminates the forest, and the mixture, now translucent, comes away from the sides of the saucepan and forms a ball around the spoon. If it doesn't, continue cooking for a few more minutes.

◆ Add the rose water and cook for another 5 minutes.

◆ Line a tray with parchment paper and sift over a thin layer of cornstarch, as fine as the gentlest snow. Carefully spread the paste over the tray and smooth the top before letting it rest at room temperature for at least 12 hours, or overnight if possible.

◆ Pour the glass of confectioners' sugar onto a plate, oil a knife, and cut the paste into 1 1/4-inch cubes. Roll the Turkish delight in the confectioners' sugar, tap off the excess, and store in an airtight container.

SWORD COAST TART

This traditional dish is enjoyed by Chaos Mages, treasure hunters of all kinds, and paladins between quests.

PREPARATION TIME • 15 mins ◆ COOKING TIME • 45 mins

INGREDIENTS • serves 4

10 1/2 oz shortcrust pastry (readymade, from your bakery/store)
2 pears
4 fl oz (1/2 cup) maple syrup
1 lb 10 oz cranberries
1 oz flour
6 oz brown sugar (demerara sugar or dark soft brown sugar)
Milk, for the glaze

◆ Weigh out 1 3/4 oz of shortcrust pastry and set it aside for the decoration. Preheat the oven to 350°F.

◆ Peel the pears, remove the seeds, then dice and place the pears in a saucepan over high heat together with the maple syrup and cranberries. Stir the mixture until the cranberries burst.

◆ Sprinkle this syrupy mixture with the flour; mix in well. Reduce the heat to medium and continue to cook, stirring occasionally, to reduce the syrup by about a third. Take the saucepan off the heat and let it cool completely.

◆ Meanwhile, use a rolling pin to roll out the pastry, lay it in a medium-sized tart pan, and prick with a fork to prevent air bubbles forming.

◆ Cover the pastry base and sides with aluminum foil, pour in some ceramic baking beans or dried beans, and bake blind for about 20 minutes.

◆ Roll out the pastry that you set aside. Cut out a dragon shape using a cookie cutter or a hand-drawn stencil cut from thin cardboard. Shape the rest of the pastry into lots of little sausages, roll them out and cut out claw shapes using a knife.

◆ Remove the beans and aluminum foil. Sprinkle the base of the tart with the brown sugar, spread over the stewed fruit. Carefully lay the pastry dragon on top, arrange the claws around the edge of the tart, brush with milk, and bake for 25 minutes. Serve hot or cold.

CHAPTER IV

BEWITCHING
POTIONS

Eternal love potion

Viviane, the Lady of the Lake, lived in the forest of Brocéliande, where she raised Lancelot. In the Arthurian legends, Merlin falls in love with her and teaches her all his secrets, including the potion for inspiring eternal love. Viviane made the potion and offered it to Merlin and, according to some, the two magicians have lived together in the forest, invisible to humans, ever since.

INGREDIENTS • serves 4

1 3/4 oz lavender flowers (from organic food stores)

4 1/2 oz honey

3½ fl oz lemon juice

INFUSION TIME • 20 mins ◆ RESTING TIME • One night

◆ When the world was already old and the forests still young, Merlin wandered through the forest of Brocéliande, admiring its beauty. It was then that he caught sight of Viviane, and became infatuated with her. Wishing to preserve Merlin's love for her, Viviane made up the potion that would keep him by her side.

◆ She began by drawing 2 pints (4 cups) of water from the Crystal lake, collecting honey from the forest, and picking lavender flowers, which she left to dry throughout the summer under the light of the moon. Finally, she obtained the fruit of the faraway lemon tree.

◆ Viviane heated the water in a cauldron and, as soon as the first bubbles appeared, she removed it from the heat and threw in the lavender, letting it infuse for 20 minutes.

◆ She strained the liquid through the finest piece of cheesecloth, then added the honey and lemon juice, stirring and softly singing her love for the wizard.

◆ Sealed in a crystal flask, she let the potion rest in the icy waters of the lake.

◆ Viviane offered the drink to Merlin and as soon as his lips touched the potion, he was captivated by her again. His only desire was to remain with her beneath the foliage of the forest, until the end of time.

Ent-draught

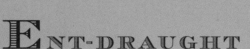

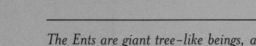

The Ents are giant tree-like beings, able to speak, think, and move. They are the ancient guardians and protectors of the forests of Middle-earth. In The Lord of the Rings, Merry and Pippin, seeking refuge in Fangorn Forest, meet Treebeard, the eldest of the Ents, who provides protection for them at Gandalf's request. This explains how, for a time, Merry and Pippin live on the mysterious Ent-draught, which makes those who drink it grow taller.

PREPARATION TIME • 15 mins ◆ RESTING TIME • 30 mins

COOKING TIME • 10 mins

INGREDIENTS • serves 4

2 1/4 lb blackberries

1 lb 2 oz blueberries

3 1/2 oz elderberry flowers and leaves (from organic food stores or the health/herbal tea section of the supermarket)

3 1/2 oz mallow leaves (from organic food stores or the health/herbal tea section of the supermarket)

7 oz maple syrup

◆ Rinse the harvested fruits, flowers, and leaves.

◆ In a pot made of clay from the Old Forest, bring 2 pints (4 cups) fresh spring water to a boil. When the first bubbles appear, add the berries and cook for 5 minutes until they burst and release their juices.

◆ Add the flowers, leaves, and maple syrup. Mix for another 5 minutes and strain the liquid through a strainer (or through the roots of an obliging Ent, if one can be found).

◆ Bottle the Ent-draught and keep in a cool place, in the icy water of a leaping stream, for example.

GANDALF'S PICK-ME-UP

Gandalf the Grey, later Gandalf the White, is the most famous wizard of Middle-earth. Renowned among the hobbits for his spectacular fireworks, he is the companion and friend first of Bilbo, then later of Frodo, Bilbo's nephew (really cousin). Gandalf guides the Fellowship of the Ring through the thousand and one perils sent by Sauron to retrieve the Ring of Power. Gandalf keeps with him a flask filled with miruvor, an elven cordial able to lift the spirits under any circumstances, including climbing the pass of Caradhras.

PREPARATION TIME • 20 mins ◆ RESTING TIME • 1 hr

◆ Gather the fruits at dawn on the summer solstice and rinse them carefully with the clear waters of the Bruinen.

◆ Cut the orange and lemon in half and squeeze to collect their juice.

◆ Remove the skin and stones of the peaches and pit the cherries, then place the fruits in a mortar (or a food processor) with the washed and de-stemmed red currants and purée them, before adding orange and lemon juice.

◆ Strain through a gossamer cloth (or a fine strainer) to obtain a clear liquid.

◆ Pour into stoppered bottles and keep in the refrigerator, until no later than the dawn of the fifth day.

INGREDIENTS • serves 4

1 orange
1 lemon
1 lb 2 oz yellow peaches
1 lb 2 oz cherries
2 lb 4 oz red currants

BEORNING BEVERAGE

On the eve of battle, the bear-men traditionally drink this mixture made of honey from their hives and cherries from their woods, which allows them to take the form of a bear. In The Hobbit, it is Beorn himself in the guise of a giant black bear who ends the Battle of Five Armies by slaying the orc chieftain.

PREPARATION TIME • 20 mins   ♦   RESTING TIME • 1 hr

COOKING TIME • 10 mins

INGREDIENTS • serves 4

2 lb 4 oz cherries
16 fl oz (2 cups) mild honey

♦ Rinse the cherries on a moonless night, remove their pits, and squeeze them through a cloth to collect their juice.

♦ Heat 16 fl oz (2 cups) water to lukewarm in a saucepan and pour in the honey. Stir gently until it melts.

♦ Add the cherry juice and heat for another 5 minutes, mixing together well.

♦ Take off the heat and cool completely. Pour the beverage into stoppered bottles and place in the refrigerator.

♦ Drink as soon as you hear the orcs approaching in the distance.

Elf-made wine (alcohol-free)

When Narcissa Malfoy and Bellatrix Lestrange visit Severus Snape, he swears an Unbreakable Vow with Narcissa, after which they drink a toast to the glory of the Dark Lord.

INGREDIENTS • serves 4

1 orange
16 fl oz (2 cups) grape juice
1 handful blueberries (frozen if out of season)
4 T soft brown sugar
1 t ground ginger
1 t ground nutmeg
1 cinnamon stick
1 star anise

PREPARATION TIME • 5 mins ◆ COOKING TIME • 5 mins

RESTING TIME • 1 hr

◆ Begin by casting an Iron-shield spell to protect your hands, then, using a very sharp knife, cut the peel from the orange. Pull apart the segments, remove the white membrane covering them, and cut the flesh into segments.
◆ Pour all the ingredients into a cauldron, beginning with the blood-colored grape juice.
◆ Add 10 fl oz (1 1/4 cups) water and boil for 5 minutes. Take the cauldron off the heat and let it rest for 1 hour. Strain and serve scalding hot or icy cold.

Memory potion

Severus Snape was extremely fond of Harry's mother, Lily Potter. After she died, he is said to have often drunk this potion, which is able to preserve memories intact.

INGREDIENTS • One 16 fl oz (2 cup) flask

3 1/2 oz ubull fruit (apple)
1 bean of melipone (vanilla)
A few phoenix tears (2 T maple syrup)
14 fl oz (1 3/4 cups) juice of lythraceae (pomegranate)

PREPARATION TIME • 20 mins

◆ This potion must be prepared in utter silence, which is impossible for dunderheads like you. I do not expect, therefore, that you will remember anything but the color of your pillow.
◆ Rinse the ubull fruit, peel it, cut it, remove the seeds, and stew it with a little water in a cauldron on a medium heat. Split the melipone bean in half, then, using your wand or the back of a knife, scrape out the inside to collect the seeds. Add the seeds to the stewed ubull and mix in.
◆ Place the phoenix tears in a second cauldron, add the stewed ubull, and pour in the juice of lythraceae. Stir three times in the direction of the wheels of a Time-Turner, then four times in the opposite direction.
◆ Let cool, bottle in a flask, and be ready to astound with your elephantine memory!

GENUINE BUTTERBEER (ALCOHOL-FREE)

Butterbeer was born in 1855 in Great Britain, with the invention of butterscotch. Combined with vanilla soda, this syrupy liquid looked so much like beer that it was nicknamed "butterbeer." Fred and George, Ron Weasley's twin brothers, were the chief suppliers for parties in the common room. Let the butterbeer flow like water!

PREPARATION TIME • 5 mins ◆ COOKING TIME • 10 mins

INGREDIENTS • serves 4

2 1/4 oz butter
2 1/4 oz superfine sugar
1 T molasses or golden syrup
(international foods section of your store)
16 fl oz (2 cups) cream soda or vanilla soda (online or in the international foods section)
Whipped cream, to your heart's content

◆ Melt the butter in a small cauldron over low heat, add the sugar, and stir gently. Cast an Unstick spell or use a damp brush to remove any sugar crystals that stick to the sides. Use a Levitation spell and add the molasses or golden syrup. Boil for 5 minutes.
◆ Let the mixture cool completely or cast a Chill spell. Pour 2 tablespoons of syrup into each mug, then add some cream soda. Top with a generous dose of whipped cream and enjoy.

WARM BUTTERBEER (ALCOHOL-FREE)

Served warm, butterbeer is a cheering drink after trudging through the snow in Hogsmeade or for giving you the strength to fight the forces of evil.

INGREDIENTS • serves 4

2 1/4 oz butter
2 1/4 oz superfine sugar
1 T molasses or golden syrup
(international foods section of your store)
16 fl oz (2 cups) milk
Whipped cream, to your heart's content

PREPARATION TIME • 5 mins ◆ COOKING TIME • 5 mins

◆ Follow step 1 of the cold butterbeer recipe (without cooling the syrup).
◆ Pour in the milk and warm the mixture, stirring gently. Serve in mugs and top with whipped cream according to your preference.

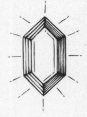

GREEN POTION

In the world of Hyrule, this potion allows Link to restore his powers.

INGREDIENTS • 2 pt flask (4 cups)

16 fl oz (2 cups) waterfall water
16 fl oz (2 cups) kiwifruit juice
4 T cherry syrup
Juice of 1 lemon
1 handful maraschino cherries

PREPARATION TIME • 5 mins ◆ RESTING TIME • 15 mins

◆ In one of the Secret Caves of Hyrule, known to the Fairies yet unknown to the Octoroks, pour the water from a waterfall through a magic flute into a cauldron.

◆ Add the kiwifruit juice given to you by the Minish on your last quest and stir gently.

◆ Pour the cherry syrup into a pitcher, and add the the lemon juice and the kiwifruit mixture.

◆ Add the maraschino cherries and let the potion rest for 15 minutes to restore the maximum number of magic points, before decanting into your flask.

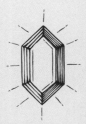

"SUPERCALIFRAGILISTICEXPIALIDOCIOUS" ELIXIR

A very exclusive cocktail, served by penguin waiters on Derby Day.

PREPARATION TIME • 15 mins

◆ Chip some small chunks of ice from an iceberg. Divide them between 4 glasses. Divide the cherry syrup, grapefruit juice, peach juice, and vanilla extract equally between the glasses.

◆ Stir gently with Mary Poppins' umbrella and enjoy while watching the carousel horse race.

INGREDIENTS • serves 4

4 T cherry syrup
8 fl oz (1 cup) grapefruit juice
1 1/2 pt (3 cups) peach juice
2 t vanilla extract

Dragon potion

This will allow you, like the vengeful Maleficent, to wake up or put to sleep your inner dragon.

PREPARATION TIME • 5 mins

◆ When the tempest breaks and the storm rises, pour the essence of terror into a goblet, watching it shimmer in the flashes of lightning.

◆ At the second clap of thunder, add your wounded pride and concentrated vengeance. Smile your darkest smile and stir with your scepter.

◆ When gusts of wind start whirling around you, it is time to add the juice of the fire fruit. Then drink and unleash your terrible wrath.

INGREDIENTS • serves 4

Essence of terror
(or 4 T blue curaçao syrup)
wounded pride
(or 16 fl oz [2 cups] apple juice)
Concentrated vengeance
(or 16 fl oz/2 cups cranberry juice)
Fire fruit
(or the juice of 1 lemon)

THE WITCH-QUEEN'S BEAUTY POTION

A potion to stay forever beautiful, not to mention devious. Ha! ha! ha!

PREPARATION TIME • 15 mins ◆ COOKING TIME • 10 mins

INFUSION TIME • 15 mins

◆ Don your favorite and most flattering accessories (accursed cape, demonic scepter . . .), roll up your sleeves, then rinse and peel the pastinaca roots and slice them into rounds.

◆ Boil them for 10 minutes in a small cauldron, then strain and reserve the liquid (you can give the vegetable slices to your pet raven; it will love them).

◆ Return the strained liquid to your cauldron and mix in the ubull juice over low heat.

◆ Stir gently with your left hand the number of days in your birthday (three times if you were born on the third, and so on).

◆ Once the mixture is warm, add the hope of a simpering princess and the smile of an idiot prince, then sprinkle with the toasted powdered sleeping beauties, add the salagama bark, and let it infuse for 15 minutes before removing from the heat.

◆ This potion can be drunk hot, warm, or cold.

INGREDIENTS • One 16 fl oz (2 cup) flask

Roots of pastinaca
(or 14 fl oz [1 3/4 cups] carrot juice)
Juice of ubull
(or 3 1/2 fl oz unpoisoned apple juice)
Powder of sleeping beauties
(or 1 T ground toasted hazelnuts)
Bark of salagama
(or 1 cinnamon stick)

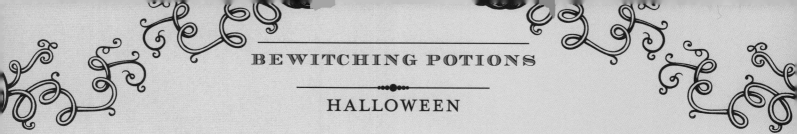

Pumpkin juice

The must-have drink for all sorcerers' gatherings!

INGREDIENTS • 1 pitcher

9 oz cooked pumpkin, squash,
butternut (frozen, if out of season)
2 pt (4 cups) apple juice
4 1/2 oz apricot jam
1 tip cinnamon stick (= 1 pinch)

PREPARATION TIME • 5 mins

◆ When the sun throws out its final rays and the Night of Ghosts and Sorcerers begins, put on your finest ceremonial apparel (although in some faraway countries, sorcerers make this recipe in their pajamas and slippers) and take up your wand.

◆ Pour the cooked pumpkin into a medium-sized cauldron (note the characteristic "plop" of the mashed pumpkin falling into the cauldron), then add the apple juice.

◆ Adjust the glasses on the end of your nose, move the toad and the cat out of the way, cast a Muffling spell so you don't draw too much attention to yourself, pick up a stick blender, and purée the mixture very thoroughly.

◆ Gradually add the apricot jam, blending in well each time. Remove the bits of pumpkin from your glasses, hair, table, and carpet.

◆ Adjust the cinnamon to your taste, decant into a pitcher, and place in the refrigerator (keep it out of reach of the toad, an orange batrachian might come as a surprise to the neighbors).

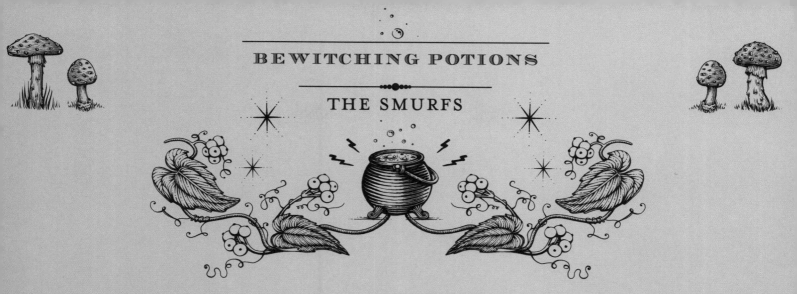

SMURFESQUE COCKTAIL

Although sarsaparilla is the Smurfs' favorite food, when it is out of season these small blue people just love to slurp a smurfesque cocktail.

INGREDIENTS • serves 4

16 fl oz (2 cups) pear juice
16 fl oz (2 cups) soda water
4 T curaçao
1 handful raspberries
4 cinnamon sticks

PREPARATION TIME • 10 mins

◆ When the whole village is gathered together and the sun is shining high in the sky, slowly smurf* the pear juice into glasses.

◆ Next, smurf** the smurfling*** water and smurf**** without letting Brainy Smurf break your concentration.

◆ When the mixture fizzes, smurf***** the curaçao down the inside of the glass: it must reach the very bottom without dissmurfing******.

◆ Then, and only then, smurf******* the raspberries that you have smurfly saved from Greedy Smurf.

◆ Stir with a cinnamon stick and sip, smurfing gaily.

*pour   **add   ***soda   ****stir   *****dribble   ******dissolving   *******quickly add

MESOPOTAMIAN NECTAR

My dearest Ptolemy, you are my master and the only magician who did not simply rule but also sought to truly understand us djinn—including me, Bartimaeus, although I am, it is true, especially special. Anyway, as I was saying, one day while enjoying this beverage, Ptolemy made me promise to be a little more discreet and to avoid trouble in the future. . . . I did manage it, at least for four days.

PREPARATION TIME • 5 mins

◆ Shell and roughly crush the pistachios. Turn yourself into a dragon and toast them with a single breath, or toast in a pan over medium heat for 1 to 2 minutes.

◆ Half-fill four glasses with ice cubes.

◆ Divide the rose syrup between the glasses (only use syrup made from flowers from the Hanging Gardens of Babylon, or, if you must, Damask roses: the others aren't worth a pentacle).

◆ Casually fling a handful of crushed pistachios and pine nuts into each glass and pour over the grape juice.

◆ Yes, I know, it's excellent. . . . No, no, don't thank me. . . . Worshipping me will be quite enough, no really, I assure you!

INGREDIENTS • serves 4

2 3/4 oz unsalted pistachios
Ice cubes
3 T rose syrup
1 T pine nuts
16 fl oz (2 cups) grape juice

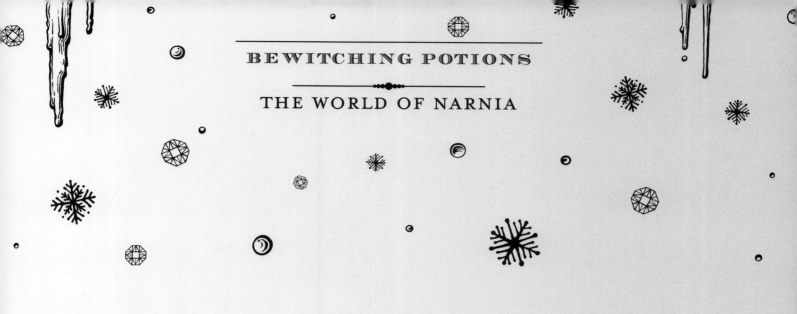

DIGORY'S SECRET (see photo on page 170)

Digory and his friend Polly were the first children to visit Narnia and meet the White Witch. It happened completely by accident—they were in the attic, innocently drinking ginger beer, but who knows what will happen when you are also playing with magic rings.

PREPARATION TIME • 5 mins ◆ INFUSION TIME • 15 mins

◆ Peel the ginger root and cut it into thin slices.

◆ Pour the apple juice into a cauldron and warm it over medium heat, add the pieces of ginger root, turn off the heat and let it infuse for 15 minutes, and then strain and reserve the liquid.

◆ Let the strained ginger and apple juice cool completely.

◆ Divide the crushed ice between the glasses, then add some ginger and apple juice to each. Add 4 1/4 fl oz (1/2 cup) water to each glass and a few rounds of lemon, and stir using a cinnamon stick.

◆ Raise a toast to Aslan, empty your glass, and jump into the ring to discover the Wood between the Worlds!

INGREDIENTS • serves 4

1 ginger root
16 fl oz (2 cups) apple juice
1 T crushed ice
1 lemon, sliced into rounds
4 cinnamon sticks

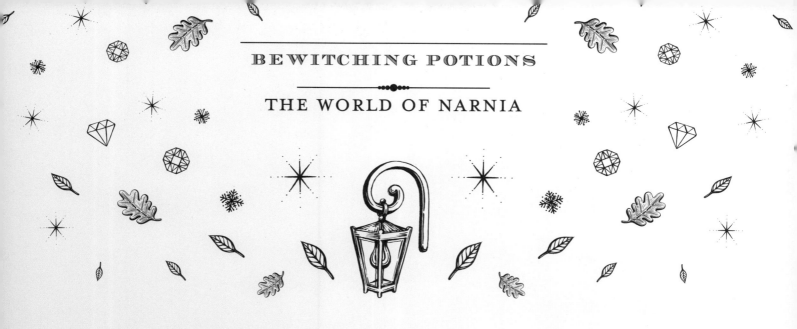

THE COMFORT OF THE WHITE WITCH

After meeting the White Witch of Narnia, Edmund Pevensie is so cold he is unable to speak. Jadis gives him this comforting magical beverage and Edmund soon forgets the icy conditions that reign in Narnia, where it is always winter yet never Christmas.

INGREDIENTS • serves 4

1 1/2 pt (3 cups) milk
8 fl oz (1 cup) decaffeinated coffee
1 can whipped cream
4 T unsweetened cocoa powder

The caramel
9 oz light soft brown sugar
½ T white vinegar

PREPARATION TIME • 5 mins ◆ COOKING TIME • 15 mins

◆ Make the caramel before the cold turns you solid and you become one of the statues at the castle of Jadis the White Witch. In a large saucepan, melt the brown sugar with 1/3 cup of water and the vinegar over high heat, then bring to a boil, constantly stirring with a wooden spoon. As soon as the first bubbles appear, lower the heat. If, like snowflakes on a window, sugar crystals stick to the side of your saucepan, melt them with your damp brush.

◆ Place your saucepan in the sink and, being very careful of any spatter, pour 1/3 cup water onto the caramel. Wait until the bubbles calm down and return the saucepan to low heat for 1 minute, stirring.

◆ Let the caramel cool completely before decanting into a crystal flask.

◆ Place a saucepan over very low heat, mix together the milk, 3 oz of the newly made caramel, and the coffee, stirring frequently.

◆ Pour into cups, top generously with whipped cream, sprinkle with cocoa, and serve very hot. Use the remaining homemade caramel to drizzle over each drink and decorate.

GRAND VIZIER

Being a villain can go to your head but sometimes Jafar needs to clear his before embarking on another round of sinister plots and dark designs. The Grand Vizier is a drink as unique as Jafar—its recipe has remained a secret . . . until today.

PREPARATION TIME • 10 mins   ◆   COOKING TIME • 5 mins

RESTING TIME • 15 mins

INGREDIENTS • serves 4

1 pinch of chili powder
1 t fennel seeds (or 2 herbal teabags)
2 t mustard
1 t turmeric
3 1/2 oz soy milk
Salt

◆ Bring 2 pints (4 cups) of water to a boil, then add the spices in the following order: the chili to clarify your mind, the fennel for coming up with devious schemes, the velvety mustard to solidify your ideas, and the turmeric because gold is the only color worthy of me!
◆ Remove from the heat and let the spices infuse for 10 minutes while reciting the names on your grudge list. Take a break (it's a long list). Strain the liquid into a pitcher, add the soy milk, taste, season with salt, and put in the refrigerator for 15 minutes before serving.
◆ Well? Unique, don't you think?

GENIE ELIXIR

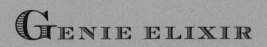

A drink to make you fit to face a rage–filled Vizier while tap dancing and tickling the ears of the Sultan!

INGREDIENTS • serves 4

4 T blueberry jelly
10 fl oz (1 1/4 cups) raspberry juice
16 fl oz (2 cups) apple juice
Juice of 1 lemon

PREPARATION TIME • 5 mins

◆ When confronted with a powerful enemy, try this elixir fix. Divide the blueberry jelly between 4 glasses. Pour the raspberry juice, apple juice, and lemon juice into a pitcher and stir.
◆ Divide the fruit juice between the glasses and arm yourself with this elixir when Jafar is about to explode with wrath. He may be a wizard, but he had better hold tight onto to his curly-toed slippers!

Magic potion

Perhaps the most famous potion of them all! A classic, producing many different magical effects, including giving the drinker superhuman strength, lending speech to the the voiceless, and reviving the unconscious. It even makes daisies bloom more quickly! But be careful not to fall into a cauldron full of it!

INGREDIENTS • serves 4

7 fl oz blueberry juice
1 T baking soda
2 3/4 oz superfine sugar
Juice of 4 lemons
1 T juice from freshly picked carrots
5 fl oz (2/3 cup) strawberry juice
1 T beet juice
Honey to taste

PREPARATION TIME • 10 mins   •   RESTING TIME • 5 mins

◆ A warning from Obelix: "Getafix wants me to tell you to make absolutely sure no one falls into the cauldron of potion, blah blah blah . . ."

◆ Heat the blueberry juice and 1/3 cup water in a small cauldron sheltered from the wind, and, if possible, under an oak tree at least one hundred years old and home to a family of chickadees (their birdsong is ideal for concentration). Next, blend the baking soda and sugar into the liquid in the cauldron.

◆ When the mixture is the color of a moonless night (very dark blue), add all the lemon juice at once and mix enthusiastically. Your potion should start to bubble up; and if its color goes from dark blue to ruby red, you will have earned your druid's sickle!

◆ Next, add the carrot juice drop by drop, stirring as you go, the strawberry juice all at once, and the beet juice half a spoonful at a time; stir gently. Taste, and add as much honey as you please.

◆ Now you are ready for a new adventure!

◆ Druid tip: "If it be not the season of the blueberry, the same quantity of the juice of the black currant will suffice."

Invisibility potion

Allowing you, as its name suggests, to become invisible, this potion is very useful for hiding from adversaries in battle, listening at doors, or stealing a magical item. Be careful though, only your body is invisible, not your shadow.

PREPARATION TIME • 2 mins ◆ RESTING TIME • 10 mins

INGREDIENTS • 2 pt (4 cup) bottle

◆ Juice the fruits without losing a drop, or someone might suspect what you are up to. Blend the syrup of trompe l'oeil with the juices of Intentions and Irony, then add the Fizzing Spirit of Troll. Rinse the leaves of Discretion and add to the potion. Let it infuse for 10 minutes, then strain into a bottle.
◆ If you venture into caves illuminated by ultraviolet light, keep in mind that your potion will become phosphorescent and thus be able to light your way, but also betray your presence . . .

2 Fruits of Intention (or 2 limes)

1 pt (2 cups) Juice of Irony
(or yellow grapefruit juice)

6 T Syrup of Trompe-l'œil
(or cane sugar syrup)

1 pt (2 cups) Fizzing Spirit of Troll
(or tonic water)

1 Hint of Discretion
(or a sprig of mint)

Friendly arm inn hippocras

There's nothing like a good tankard of hippocras to restore the spirits after taking on obstreperous giants, ill-tempered magicians, zombies, ghouls, and other nefarious shadows.

PREPARATION TIME • 5 mins ◆ RESTING TIME • 3 hrs

INGREDIENTS • serves 4

◆ Peel and grate the ginger root. Pound together the cardamom pods and cloves, add the ground cinnamon, and mix with the ginger. Warm the grape juice in a small cauldron over low heat, blend in the honey, then add the spices.
◆ Turn off the heat and let infuse for the time it takes to undo the Confusion spell you accidentally cast over the mage's wyvern near the door. Let 2 to 3 hours pass.
◆ Strain the hippocras into a pitcher and offer to buy everyone a round of drinks so no one notices your friends escape via the secret passage under the counter.

2 1/4 oz fresh ginger root

10 cardamom pods

10 cloves

1 oz ground cinnamon

2 pt (4 cups) red grape juice

6 t dark honey (chestnut or fir)

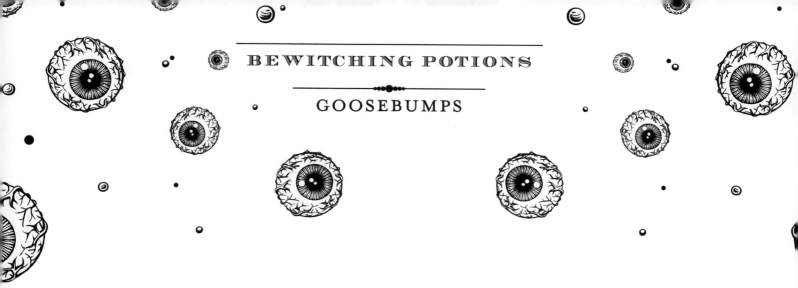

SLAPPY'S GHOSTLY PUNCH

When Slappy the Dummy releases the monsters from the various Goosebumps books, he thinks victory will be easy. He doesn't count on the author and his friends, who soon manage to reduce The Blob that Ate Everyone to mush, trapping bits of zombie along the way.

PREPARATION TIME • 5 mins   ♦   FREEZING TIME • 3 hrs

INGREDIENTS • serves 8

4 sheets gelatin
4 oranges
2 pt (4 cups) raspberry juice
2 pt (4 cups) strawberry juice
4 T blackberry jelly
4 T honey
2 sprigs mint

♦ Heat 2 pints (4 cups) water in a small cauldron, without letting it come to a boil, then dissolve the sheets of gelatin in it. Rinse a pair of latex gloves, making sure to remove all traces of talcum powder.

♦ When the gelatin has dissolved, completely fill the latex gloves with this water, tie a knot at the wrist, making it tight so the water can't escape, and place the gloves in the refrigerator for at least 3 hours.

♦ Squeeze the oranges, and mix the juice with the raspberry and strawberry juices in a clear crystal bowl.

♦ Spread the blackberry jelly in small bowls or one large bowl, pour the juice down the sides of the bowl, followed by the honey.

♦ Take the gloves out of the refrigerator, cut the latex at the knot and carefully unmold the ice. Place the frozen hands in the bowl, crush the mint between your fingers, throw it around the frozen hands, and serve.

INDEX

Find all the sorcerers' worlds and their corresponding recipes in My Who's Who of Sorcerers on page 8.

BIBLIOGRAPHY

GENERAL

- LOISEAU, Bernard, GILBERT, Gérard, *Trucs, astuces et tours de main*, Hachette, 1996.
- BOTTÉRO, Jean, *La plus vieille cuisine du monde*, Éditions Louis Audibert, 2002.
- MATHIOT, Ginette, *Merveilles de la cuisine internationale et exotique*, Flammarion, 1967.
- MASSIALOT, François, *Le cuisinier roïal et bourgeois*, Chez Claude Prudhomm, 1691.
  Available here: http://gallica.bnf.fr/ark:/12148/bpt6k108571q

SORCERERS IN PRINT

- COLLECTIF, *50 contes et histoires enchantées*, Compagnie Internationale du Livre, 1980.
- PERRAULT, Charles, *Contes*, Hachette, collection Grandes Oeuvres, 1978.
- ANDERSEN, Hans Christian, *The Little Mermaid & Other Stories*, Hachette, collection Grandes Oeuvres, 1992.
- GRIMM, Jacob, GRIMM, Wilhelm, *Grimm's Fairy Tales*, Auzou, 2011.
- LEPRINCE DE BEAUMONT, Jeanne-Marie, D'AULNOY, Marie-Catherine,
  La Belle et la Bête et autres contes, Le Livre de Poche Jeunesse, 1979.
- CAMIGLIERI, Laurence, *Contes et Légendes du Poitou et des Charentes*,
  coll. Contes et Légendes de tous les pays, Fernand Nathan, 1977.
- COLLECTIF, *Contes et Légendes de Brocéliande*, Terre de Brume, 2000.
- SHAKESPEARE, William, *A Midsummer Night's Dream*, Le Livre de Poche, 1983.
- DAHL, Roald, *The Witches*, Gallimard, collection 1000 Soleils, 1984.
- BAUM, L. Frank, *The Wizard of Oz*, J'ai Lu, 1993.
- TRAVERS, P. L., *Mary Poppins*, Hachette, collection jeunesse, 1980.
- ROWLING, J. K., *Fantastic Beasts & Where to Find Them*, Gallimard Jeunesse, 2001.
- BARKS, Carl, *Les Trésors de Picsou*, Disney Hachette Presse, 2006–2014.
- STINE, R. L., *Goosebumps* series, Bayard Poche, collection Passion de Lire, 1998–2001.
- CLARKE, GILSON, François, *Melusine series*, Dupuis, 1995–2016.
- GOSCINNY, René, UDERZO, Albert, FERRI, Jean-Yves, *Asterix* series,
  Dargaud, Albert & René, Hachette, 1959–2016.
- PEYO, *Les Schtroumpfs* series, Dupuis puis Le Lombard, 1963–2016.
- BRAND, Christianna, *Nurse Matilda*, Knight, 1975.
- TEZUKA, Osamu, *Le Roi Léo*, Glénat Manga, 1996.

THE LORD OF THE RINGS

- TOLKIEN, J. R. R., *The Hobbit*, Le Livre de Poche, 1980.
- TOLKIEN, J. R. R., *The Lord of the Rings*, Volume 1: The Fellowship of the Ring, Presse Pocket, 1986.
- TOLKIEN, J. R. R., *The Lord of the Rings*, Volume 2: The Two Towers, Presse Pocket, 1991.
- TOLKIEN, J. R. R., *The Lord of the Rings*, Volume 3: The Return of the King, Presse Pocket, 1991.

THE BARTIMAEUS TRILOGY

- STROUD, Jonathan, Volume 1: *The Amulet of Samarkand*, Livre de Poche Jeunesse, 2010.
- STROUD, Jonathan, Volume 2: *The Golem's Eye*, Livre de Poche Jeunesse, 2008.
- STROUD, Jonathan, Volume 3: *Ptolemy's Gate*, Livre de Poche Jeunesse, 2011.
- STROUD, Jonathan, Prequel to the trilogy: *The Ring of Solomon*, Livre de Poche Jeunesse, 2013.

LES PARIS DES MERVEILLES SERIES

• PEVEL, Pierre, *Les Enchantements d'Ambremer*, Bragelonne, 2015.
• PEVEL, Pierre, *L'Élixir d'Oubli*, Bragelonne, 2015.
• PEVEL, Pierre, *Le Royaume Immobile*, Bragelonne, 2015.

HARRY POTTER

• ROWLING, J. K., *Harry Potter and the Philosopher's Stone*, Gallimard, 1999.
• ROWLING, J. K., *Harry Potter and the Chamber of Secrets*, Gallimard, 1999.
• ROWLING, J. K., *Harry Potter and the Prisoner of Azkaban*, Gallimard, 1999.
• ROWLING, J. K., *Harry Potter and the Goblet of Fire*, Gallimard, 2000.
• ROWLING, J. K., *Harry Potter and the Order of the Phoenix*, Gallimard, 2003.
• ROWLING, J. K., *Harry Potter and the Half-Blood Prince*, Gallimard, 2005.
• ROWLING, J. K., *Harry Potter and the Deathly Hallows*, Gallimard, 2007.

THE CHRONICLES OF NARNIA

• LEWIS, C. S., *The Magician's Nephew*, coll. Folio Junior, Gallimard Jeunesse, 2001.
• LEWIS, C.S., *The Lion, the Witch and the Wardrobe*, coll. Bibliothèque du Chat Perché, Flammarion, 1980.
• LEWIS, C. S., *Prince Caspian: The Return to Narnia*, coll. Castor Poche, Flammarion, 1993.
• LEWIS, C. S., *The Horse and His Boy*, coll. Folio Junior, Gallimard Jeunesse, 2001.
• LEWIS, C. S., *The Voyage of the Dawn Treader*, coll. Bibliothèque du Chat Perché, Flammarion, 1983.
• LEWIS, C. S., *The Silver Chair*, coll. Bibliothèque du Chat Perché, Flammarion, 1984.
• LEWIS, C. S., *The Last Battle*, coll. Folio Junior, Gallimard Jeunesse, 2002.

SORCERERS ON THE SMALL AND LARGE SCREEN

• *The Sword in the Stone*, Wolfgang Reitherman, Disney Studios, 1963.
• *Willow*, Ron Howard; Imagine Entertainment, Lucasfilm, Metro-Goldym-Mayer, 1988.
• *The Lion King*, Rob Minkoff, Roger Allers, Disney Studios, 1994.
• *Nanny McPhee*, Kirk Jones, Universal Pictures, 2006.
• *Goosebumps*, Rob Letterman, Columbia Pictures, 2015.
• *Doctor Strange*, Scott Derrickson, Marvel Studios, 2016.
• *Fantastic Beasts and Where to Find Them*, David Yates, Warner Bros, 2016.
• *Warcraft*, Duncan Jones, Legendary Pictures, Universal Pictures, 2016.
• *Bewitched*, Wiliam Asher for ABC, 1964–1972.
• *Ulysses 31*, Jean Chalopin, Nina Wolmark; DIC, Tokyo Movie Shinsha, 1981–1982.
• *Kaamelott*, Alexandre Astier, François Guérin, Calt, 2004–2009.

GAMES

• *Dungeons & Dragons*, Tactical Studies Rules and Wizards of the Coast, 1974–2016.
• *The Legend of Zelda*, Nintendo, 1986–2016.
• *World of Warcraft*, Blizzard Entertainment, 1994–2016.
• *Baldur's Gate*, Tales of the Sword Coast, Icewind Dale, BioWare and Black Isle Studios, 1998–2012.

Alexia would like to thank everyone who helped in styling the images:
· Marion Dupuis the witch for her precious assistance
and Smurf-like technical skills. A thousand thank yous!
· Romain the young Padawan.

And the following people for lending props,
each more bizarre than the last:
· Julien and Eugénie the forest wizards.
· TEO LEO Gallery (www.teoleo-galerie.com).

And, finally, thank you to Marjorie, Corinne, and Didier for their trust.